The Intimate Edge

*Extending the Reach of
Psychoanalytic Interaction*

Darlene Bregman Ehrenberg, Ph.D.

W. W. Norton & Company • New York • London

Printed in the United States of America.

First Edition

The text of this book was composed in English Times. Composition by
Bytheway Typesetting Services, Inc. Manufacturing by Haddon
Craftsmen, Inc. Book design by Justine Burkat Trubey.

Library of Congress Cataloging-in-Publication Data

Ehrenberg, Darlene Bregman.
    The intimate edge : extending the reach of psychoanalytic
interaction / Darlene Bregman Ehrenberg.
        p.   cm.
    "A Norton professional book."
    Includes bibliographical references and index.
    ISBN 0-393-70140-9
    1. Psychotherapist and patient. 2. Countertransference
(Psychology) — Therapeutic use. 3. Transference (Psychology) —
Therapeutic use. 4. Psychoanalysis. I. Title.
    [DNLM: 1. Countertransference (Psychology) 2. Psychoanalysis.
WM 460 E33i]
RC480.8.E37 1992
616.89′17 — dc20
DNLM/DLC   92-12790 CIP

W.W. Norton & Company, Inc., 500 Fifth Avenue, New York, N.Y. 10110
W.W. Norton & Company, Ltd., 10 Coptic Street, London WC1A 1PU

7 8 9 0

A NORTON PROFESSIONAL BOOK

To Jonathan and Erica

Contents

iv

Acknowledgments

THE PSYCHOANALYTIC RELATIONSHIP is a medium for growth and an endless adventure not only for our patients but also for ourselves. I want to express my deep gratitude to my patients, for the opportunity to share in this unique and intimate experience with them, through which I have certainly grown as much as they, and for their generosity in permitting me to write about our work together.

I also want to express my appreciation to Dr. Bernard Ehrenberg who always challenged me to take my thinking further and whose incisive comments often enabled me to do so, and to Drs. Arthur Feiner, Edgar Levenson, and Pearl Ellen Gordon for their sensitive readings of my papers over many years, for their valuable comments and suggestions, and for their encouragement and support. Dr. Arthur Feiner, as editor of *Contemporary Psychoanalysis*, where many of my papers have been published, was especially generous with his editorial expertise.

Thanks also to Drs Irwin Hoffman, Joyce McDougall and Christopher Bollas, who were helpful in many ways over many years.

Thanks to Samuel Bregman, Pauline Bregman, Dr. Alvin Bregman, and Reva Wolf.

Thanks to Susan Barrows Munro, from whose elegant style I learned a great deal.

I am also grateful to so many other friends and colleagues for their thoughtful comments on my work and for their interest and encouragement. The William Alanson White Institute provided a unique environment for analytic growth, and Division 39, The Division of Psychoanalysis of the American Psychological Association, provided an opportunity for dialogue with analysts of many backgrounds and points of view.

Thanks to Dorothy Bender, Dr. Jay Kwawer, Dr. Jonathan Slavin, Pascale and David Henrickson, and Dr. Marc Siegert, for their generous computer assistance.

The clinical data I will present spans a twenty-two year period of experience in private practice and reflects the evolution of my own way of working and thinking over this period.

Some of the following chapters are revised and expanded versions of papers previously published in *Contemporary Psychoanalysis*. The changes in the first two reflect the way my thinking has evolved in the years since they were written.

Chapter 3, The "Intimate Edge," is based on "The 'intimate edge' in therapeutic relatedness," *Contemporary Psychoanalysis*, 1974, 10: 423–437.

Chapter 6, Dangers of Countertransference Resistance, is based on "Countertransference resistance," *Contemporary Psychoanalysis*, 1985a, 21: 563–576.

Chapter 8, Playfulness, is based on "Playfulness in the psychoanalytic relationship," *Contemporary Psychoanalysis*, 1990 26: 74–95.

Chapter 10, "Abuse and Desire" is a much expanded version of a paper entitled "Abuse and desire: A case of father-daughter incest," *Contemporary Psychoanalysis*, 1987. It includes extensive material describing my work with a male victim of sexual abuse which has not been published before.

Material from several other papers listed in the References (Ehrenberg 1975, 1976, 1982a,b, 1984a, b, 1985b) has been used in varying ways throughout this book.

our can'ts were born to happen
our mosts have died in more

e. e. cummings

Introduction

PSYCHOANALYSTS OF DIVERSE orientations increasingly have come to recognize that patient and analyst are continually influencing and being influenced by each other in a dialectical way, often without awareness. This has radical implications for theory of psychoanalytic technique. Where these psychoanalysts disagree is in their conceptions of what the specific implications of an interactive view of the analytic field might be.

Despite these differences, which occur *within* as well as between the diverse analytic traditions,[1] I believe an interactive view of the analytic field has some theoretical and technical implications that bridge all psychoanalytic perspectives and which cannot be ignored by any of them. In this book I will elaborate my views on these issues and present the results of my own clinical explorations as to specific ways awareness of these might help us refine our ways of working.

My premise is that the recognition that analyst and patient simply *cannot* avoid having an impact on each other, even if both are totally silent, requires us to realize that even if a treatment is productive or successful, we cannot be clear whether this is related to our deliberate technical interventions or to aspects of the interaction that have eluded our awareness.

For this reason I will suggest that it is useful and necessary *to distinguish between theory of technique, which relates to what we do with awareness and intention, and theory of therapeutic action, which has to do with what is healing in the psychoanalytic interaction whether or not it evolves from our "technique."*[2]

I believe that recognizing this can allow us to expand our knowledge of the complex and subtle factors that account for therapeutic action. This can ultimately become the most effective basis for refining and developing our understanding of how to best use ourselves to advance the analytic work and to facilitate more profound and incisive kinds of psychoanalytic engagement, no matter what our theoretical orientation.

An appreciation of the power of interactive forces in the analytic field not only challenges many of the traditionally held beliefs about the nature of therapeutic action, but also requires us to recognize the untenability of the traditional view that the analyst can be an objective participant in the work. It helps us to grasp the extent to which presumably therapeutic interpretations, for example, can be ways of harassing, demeaning, patronizing, impinging on, penetrating, or violating the patient, or ways of gratifying, supporting, complying, among a multitude of other possibilities. Where patient and analyst assume that the analyst is in a position to be an *objective* interpreter of the patient's experience, this may actually reflect a form of collusive enactment and a convergence of the needs of both to see the analyst as an authority. If patient and analyst both have needs to believe that the analyst is the omniscient other or the benevolent authority to which one can entrust oneself, the structure of the relationship might serve to obscure recognition of the fact that such a drama is being enacted. In this regard, Winnicott (1969) has noted that there are times when "analyses" can serve as holding operations and become interminable, without any real growth occurring.

An interactive perspective also helps to clarify why in some instances the analyst's "abstinence" carries as much risk of negative iatrogenic consequences as does active intervention. Although silence at times obviously can be respectful and facilitating, at other times it can be cruel and sadistic, or it can be based on fear of engagement, among a host of possible other meanings and functions. The contextual meanings of the patient's free association also have to be reconsidered from such a perspective. Usually viewed as the medium of analytic work, free association may at times be a profound form of resistance, a way to avoid rather than engage in an analytic process. Alternatively it can reflect a form of compliance or collusion, conscious or unconscious, with the analyst's needs, fears, resistances.

The need to clarify the contextual significance of "transference," and what it serves to achieve, or prevent, or avoid, also becomes apparent. For example, relating to the analyst on the basis of some preconceived fantasy, rather than as the person he or she is, can function to prevent the possibility of engaging meaningfully and experiencing the anxiety a more mutual and intimate engagement might arouse.

An appreciation of interactive factors also allows us to consider that, to whatever degree the patient's perceptions of the analyst are plausible and even valid (see Ferenczi, 1933; Little, 1951; Levenson, 1972; Searles, 1975; Gill, 1982a; Hoffman, 1983), this may be due to the patient's expertise at stimulating precisely this kind of responsiveness in the analyst. The reverse is true as well. Thus, though patient and analyst each will have unique vulnerabilities, sensitivities, strengths, and needs, we must consider why particular qualities or sensitivities of either patient or analyst are activated at a given moment and not at others. At any moment patient or analyst might be involved in some kind of collusive enactment (see Racker, 1957, 1968; Levenson, 1972, 1983; Sandler, 1976, the literature on projective identification, including the work of Bion, 1967, 1983; Ogden, 1979, Grotstein, 1981, among others, as well as McDougall, 1979, on primitive forms of communication). These considerations help to illuminate why clinicians often seem to practice in ways that contradict their own stated beliefs and theoretical positions.

The powerful impact of unwitting communication between patient and analyst is, of course, one of the reasons the analyst's countertransference experience can be a source of vital data about the patient and may become the "key" to understanding aspects of the interaction that might otherwise remain impenetrable (see Heimann, 1950).

An appreciation of interactive factors also requires us to reconsider what constitutes an analytic "mistake." In this regard Winnicott (1956, 1963a) has expressed the view that there are times when our patients *need* us to fail.

> In the end the patient uses the analyst's failures, often quite small ones, perhaps manoeuvered by the patient. . . . The operative factor is that the patient now hates the analyst for the failure that originally came as an environmental factor, outside the infant's area of omnipotent control, that is *now* staged in the transference.
>
> So in the end we succeed by failing — failing the patient's way. This is a long distance from the simple theory of cure by corrective experience. (Winnicott, 1963a, p. 258)

Fromm-Reichmann (1939, 1950, 1952), has emphasized that at times the analyst's mistakes may become the basis for a "golden (analytic) opportunity." From this vantage point we might consider that how an analyst deals with his or her own inevitable fallibility may actually be one of the defining aspects of his or her technique.

An appreciation of interactive considerations thus requires us to rethink important issues of technique as well as the question of how we define "analysis." It also requires us to consider that the patient's so-called "analyzability" may be more a function of the nature of the analyst's participation than has previously been recognized. The dilemma is how to move into a new mode of thinking about clinical technique that is not beset by the inherent limitations of traditional thinking or by those of more radical new perspectives.

My focus in the chapters following will be on specific ways an appreciation of the interactive nature of the analytic field can help us to expand our understanding of the potential for therapeutic action of the analytic relationship and can enable us to refine psychoanalytic theory, and ourselves as its instrument, so as to expand the limits of what can be achieved with *all* patients through analytic work.

The Intimate Edge

CHAPTER 1

The Awakening of Desire

IN MY EXPERIENCE MANY PATIENTS seem to enter treatment suffering from what seems to be a "denial of desire." They present themselves as walking zombies, living a living death, incapable of feeling, caring, wanting, and as a result unable to relate to others; yet they seem to end up terrified by the extent of their own deadness and isolation, sometimes feeling extreme degrees of anxiety or suffering varying kinds of psychosomatic reactions.

With these patients, who have traditionally been considered "unanalyzable" and for whom traditional ways of working seem to be totally ineffective if not actually harmful, I have found that attending very closely to the immediate interaction and working at what I have described (Ehrenberg, 1974) as the "intimate edge" of the relationship is a way to begin to make contact and to have some therapeutic effect. In many such instances, focusing very painstakingly on the interaction from the beginning ultimately leads to very profound changes and to a possibility of analytic work I would not have anticipated at the outset.

What I have learned from my work with these patients has

1

helped me to appreciate even more fully the value of this way of working with all patients.

In many of the instances I am describing, what emerged over the course of our explorations was a realization of the degree to which the apparent denial of desire seemed to stem from toxic experiences and relationships, usually long-standing, in the past, particularly in early life. These relationships seemed to influence the patient's ultimate relationship to his or her own desire in profound and often devastating ways, and this in turn influenced the capacity for relationship, in a dialectical way. In some instances desire became so threatening and so painful it became too much to bear. It seemed as though for some of these patients a living death became less threatening and painful than letting themselves experience the vulnerability that is integral to experiencing any kind of hope or desire.

These observations led me to view the complex process by which an individual's unique experiential history affects his or her relation to his or her own desire as a process of "personalization" of desire through experience (Ehrenberg, 1985b). Since this in turn shapes and influences subsequent patterns of relation to others, which in turn affect the relation to desire, it began to appear that in fact what this reflects is an endless spiral of reciprocity. To the degree that this dialectical relationship between experience and desire continues throughout life, it actually becomes the basis for both positive and negative therapeutic potential: the basis for the possibility that the interpersonal experience between patient and analyst can facilitate changes in the patient's most fundamental relation to himself or herself.

The question at hand is: How can the analyst even begin to be effective where an individual's experience may have been so toxic that he or she may become closed off to all desire, and also to any kind of relationship, including and perhaps especially the analytic one? How is it possible to begin to reopen what may have become virtually a closed system? How can we begin to reach such patients so as to help them deal with their pain, their terror, and their sense of vulnerability, damage and despair, so as to facilitate the awakening of desire and a reopening to life and to relationships? How can we facilitate the mourning that will allow for the possibility of living in a healthy and full way in the present and experiencing a future that is not doomed by the past?

Let me present the results of my own efforts to grapple with these questions over many years, to illustrate how an appreciation of interactive factors within the analytic situation allows for effective ways of working with these patients.

I will begin by considering briefly the question of how extreme degrees of denial of desire and of closedness to any kind of interpersonal relation evolve. This has relevance to our thinking about how we might use ourselves more effectively in such contexts.

Whether an individual will experience his or her own desire with delight or dread, whether desire will be embraced and cherished or denied, distorted, or disavowed, whether desire remains alive and vital or alienated, will to a certain extent depend on the nature of his or her personal history and will affect his or her continuing history, *as relation to others influences relation to self, and relation to self influences what is possible with others, in an ongoing dialectical way.*

For example, where a child has been brutalized, tantalized, humiliated, even if his or her actual physical needs were met; where experience has been that communicating need or desire is likely to result in exploitation, abuse, or manipulation; or where experience has been that one's very existence is a burden to the other and evokes pain and suffering or that fulfillment of one person is always at the expense of another in a relationship,[3] the relation to desire can become quite problematic.

If an individual's history has involved traumatic experiences of frustration or abuse, seduction and betrayal, violation, exploitation, or tantalization, or where it has involved experiences of traumatic loss, anyone who arouses desire may be experienced as threatening and dangerous. The same is true where an individual has experienced his or her own uncontrollable or unchecked destructiveness. The experience of desire itself may come to be feared because desiring may be seen as being tantamount to opening oneself to the possibility of being hurt, disappointed, frustrated, exploited, or betrayed. Or it may be feared as the basis for the possibility of hurting, disappointing, frustrating, exploiting, or betraying other(s), or even of becoming rapacious, destructive, sadistic, murderous, savage, or of losing control in other ways.

Where the experience of desire may be equated with devouring or being devoured, destroying or being destroyed, contaminating or being contaminated, violating or being violated, the clinical picture often seems to involve some form of denial or repudiation of desire. For some this may take the form of a passionate desire to be able to transcend desire, to be self-sufficient and self-contained, to be able to function as a closed system. The specific defensive solutions and internal transformations that may be invoked in such contexts span a range of endless possibility.

For such individuals, the experience of desire – and thereby of need and of dependence – which is of course implicit in any use of the analysis, in any learning situation, and in any sexual relationship, may be experienced not only as dangerous but also as humiliating and threatening – a profound narcissistic injury.

Where experience has been particularly toxic, the internal dynamics in relation to the experience of desire may become so convoluted that there is no possibility of satisfaction, or even of relation, other than in sadomasochistic terms. In those instances where the prevailing desire often becomes to be self-sufficient, not dependent on another for gratification of one's needs, phenomena such as anorexia, frigidity, inability to reach orgasm, schizoid withdrawal, and even suicide are not uncommon.

Sometimes this may operate in fairly deceptive ways. With one patient, who was obese, for example, at first it seemed that the issue was voraciousness; yet analytic exploration revealed that what was actually being enacted was an effort to eliminate the experience of desire by satiating it before it could ever come into consciousness. This patient consumed to avoid experiencing desire, need or lack; she reported *never* actually experiencing hunger. Her experience was that to allow herself to feel desire was to leave herself open to terrifying and unbearable vulnerability. In fact, she described a pattern of keeping herself oversupplied so that she would never be in a position to have to feel need, desire, or dependence. Her cupboards were stocked with years' supplies of tuna fish. Her closets were filled with hundreds of shoes, pocketbooks, and dresses. She collected jewelry and art. She hoarded supplies of stationery, pencils, tape, pens. Her way of coping was to always be "provided," to never be in a position of need. She wished to be totally self-sufficient and self-contained, to transcend all dependence and vulnerability, to transcend desire, humanity, mortality, biology. In essence, she sought to transcend the human condition itself (see Becker, 1973).

In some instances the defensive denial of desire can lead to states of "psychic death." These may feel so threatening that they then provoke a desperate desire to feel desire as a confirmation of aliveness. For some patients this may take the form of drug use.

For one patient who managed to free himself of a heroin addiction, the quest for desire later took the form of pursuing women. For him the issue was not his interest in a particular woman but rather in each new woman as the bearer of a promise of evoking feelings of desire, now equated with aliveness. Ironically, the state of arousal of any desire, now symbolized by the arousal of sexual desire, came to be more desired than the state of fulfillment. This was true because in fulfillment the aliveness that was experienced by virtue of the state of arousal then eluded him.[4] The problem, of course, was that the underlying fear of any kind of dependence or gratification remained. The frustration he endlessly experienced as a result of his self-defeating patterns inevitably resulted in violent rages during which he felt out of control and which he never quite understood. These, in fact, led him to seek treatment.

The pattern of denying desire to the point of achieving a state of deadness and then desperately chasing aliveness in the form of unsatisfied desire (because satisfaction would eliminate the experience of desire) occurs in many other forms as well, all equally doomed from the outset.

For another male patient denial of desire took the form of a wish that he didn't have any genitals. His wish was not to become a woman but rather to become totally asexual, to be *"free of intense feelings that you don't have that much control over."* Not surprisingly, he was plagued by intense fears of castration. The irony in this instance was that the state of anxiety this aroused then served to reassure him of his own aliveness.

Where sexual relationships are conceived in purely sadomasochistic terms, and where sexuality may be used as a weapon in a power struggle that may be viewed in life and death terms, arousing desire or becoming the object of desire may be perceived as the way to maintain control and to protect oneself. In more extreme situations it may be used as a way humiliate, demean, abuse, or even destroy the other, and as an arena for the exercise of interpersonal power. The irony is that in such instances the very defenses meant to protect against dangers of annihilation and deprivation become devastating themselves, as these patients become controlled by them rather than the reverse. Frustration and need are perpetuated and intensified by the defensive denial of desire; this in turn refuels the toxic vicious cycle, exacerbating feelings of deprivation, rage, and vulnerability.

What is most poignant is that patients, who originally were victimized by others or by events they could not control, become victims of their own counterproductive "survival" techniques. They have resorted to states of "psychic death" to prevent what were assumed to be worse catastrophes such as disintegration, depersonalization, psychosis, multiple personality disorder, or other forms of breakdown, or at the extreme, murder or suicide.

Though such patients often present themselves as walking zombies, as incapable of feeling, loving, caring, wanting, as sexually dead, and as living an ultimately unbearable "living death," their periodic explosions, fits, losses of control, and/or psychosomatic symptoms paradoxically reveal their aliveness, even as these very symptoms can at times be life-threatening. In such instances treatment can become a matter of psychic, or even literal, life and death.

In my experience, in such instances, where traditional approaches generally not only seem inadequate to the task but may even have negative effects, sensitivity to interactive factors provides us with ways of achieving a meaningful connection and of facilitating the awakening of desire even where cynicism, terror, and despair have long prevailed. It enables us to structure the conditions of safety and help generate experiences that will be positive enough to enable even these patients, who have been severely traumatized, to feel sufficient hope to take a risk on life and on relationship.

Making *the immediate interactive experience the crucible of the work and the arena for working through* often can enable us to facilitate the awakening of desire even in individuals who seem to have long since given up wanting, feeling, and caring, as well as the willingness to risk the kind of vulnerability these imply.

DANI

Dani, a very attractive young woman in her twenties, had been anorexic and suicidal. In addition, she suffered from serious colitis and amenorrhea. She reported that she was unable to function apart from her family but felt like a "wild maniac" with them. She also described experiencing her body as separate from herself, feeling dead inside, like a robot or a machine, unable to enjoy anything including sex, incapable of orgasm, and experiencing a "living death."

At five feet six inches tall she weighed one hundred pounds. Totally preoccupied with her body and her weight, she exercised fanatically, and though she said she knew she was extremely beautiful (which she was), she felt ugly and fat. Hours each day were spent putting on makeup and trying on different clothes, after which she would inevitably end up hating how she looked. Often she was unable to go out because of this. Eating binges were standard and were typically followed by attempts to starve herself and also by taking laxatives. She would drink herself into oblivion or eat dog food to make herself sick. She would sleep with men she hated, compulsively steal things she did not need, and buy things she could not afford. Her explanation was that it was as though forces "beyond her control" took over. At times she could not distinguish between dreams and hallucinations and she found this terrifying. She insisted that her behavior had no rhyme or reason, and described feeling like a helpless bystander in relation to herself.

Her attitude toward treatment was marked by cynicism, pessimism, and despair. She was suspicious of being exploited or manipulated by me. For many months she began every session by stating that she was going to go to California instead of going through with treatment. Nevertheless, she continued to come three times a week. My focus was on the fact that she seemed to feel that all she was obliged to do was to bring her body to the sessions and the rest was up to me — and how this seemed to characterize her relation to every aspect of her life. This clarified how actively she was attempting to place the major share of the responsibility for the treatment on me and challenged her view of herself as the helpless victim. This made patently clear what she did interpersonally, which she had never quite grasped before.

As I directed my efforts toward trying to discover the logic of what she experienced as her own incomprehensible radical mood swings, I was able to relate these to specific events in our interaction. She was almost embarrassed to be "caught," as her tantrums in relation to me, her threats to destroy my office, attack other patients, and "do herself in" to get back at me could be clearly seen as the consequence of her acute sensitivity to any lapses in attention or alertness on my part.

The consequence of clarifying this was that she could no longer argue that she was a hopeless "maniac" whose behavior was beyond comprehension. She described a sense of coming out of a fog, of feeling the veil or cloud she had been submerged in was lifting.

Later, when I was a few minutes late for a session, she became distressed and agitated and would not accept my apology. She acted as though I had mortally wounded her in an unforgivable way and refused to speak the whole session.

When I noted, in the following session, how punitive she had been and told her I did not like being treated that way, she acknowledged that I could have apologized till kingdom come, but she would not have yielded. There were associations to hearing her parents in their bedroom and feeling excluded; that was how it felt when she was outside in the waiting room and I was inside my office with another patient. She then apologized to me for not accepting my apology and said it was the way she used to respond to her mother.

In one session, when it was clear that much was still unresolved and the session was about to end, she raged about the fact that I would leave her this way before a weekend and that I had *"opened her up to so much pain."* She threatened that she would go out and walk in front of a bus and kill herself if I didn't help her *"that moment."*

I told her that I did not like to be threatened. I noted also that her inability to endure any frustration seemed to be a big part of the problem. She became sheepish and conceded that she used to do this kind of thing with her parents and her boyfriends, and that usually it worked—how she used to "get away with murder." After the weekend she reported that she had held together without causing any catastrophes, but cried that it had been a great strain. She also noted that, despite all her prior treatment, only now did she realize that she would have to take responsibility for herself.

Around this time she reported an insight into a decision process when she "lost it" that was akin to *"deciding to stay on a bus even though you know you are passing your stop and you know you should get off."*

As she became increasingly aware of choices she was making as she was making them, she began to have a new perspective on some of her behavior in the past. In this context she began express remorse and regret for how awful she had been to her parents, boyfriends, siblings and me, and to struggle to develop new ways of relating. Her self-esteem increased markedly as she discovered her own capacities to be compassionate and sensitive to me, and she was appreciative of my responsiveness to her gestures. We then were able to explore the ways she had used herself as an instrument to evoke particular responses from others, often at the expense of her own needs and well-being. We learned from this that her body had become a battleground for complicated psychological dramas. Eating and not eating, for example, had become ways of pleasing and hurting others — a form of interpersonal coinage. The same applied to sex and to decisions to live or die. These had all been ways of asserting herself and of feeling she had some power, but they also came at a price and at times seemed to elude her control, so that her sense of desperation and impotence was clear. (Some of this was captured in dreams of starving in the presence of sumptuous arrays of food, of refusing to eat, and also of not being able to eat.)

As she discovered that she could express her feelings directly and be more effective, while avoiding the negative repercussions of the acting out, her symptoms abated. She stabilized her weight between one hundred ten and one hundred fifteen pounds. She also developed a romantic relationship with a young man and began to establish herself as a freelance professional.

After two years of exploring her anxieties about the work and about her intensifying relationships with me and with her boyfriend, she felt more confident and less angry and vulnerable. About this time she began to menstruate again, and after a long interval of struggling with a decision regarding whether she wanted to live with her boyfriend she decided to move in with him.

The new situation of living with her boyfriend intensified her fears of closeness and of her own vulnerability. She struggled with fears of sexual dependence and of orgasm, and was able to link these fears to the dynamics of the anorexia. That is, she resisted taking in anything as a defense against her fear of not being able to control her desires or her dependency needs if these were allowed expression. Fears of being hurt or disappointed, helplessly at the mercy of the other who might give or withhold, as well as resentment of her own feelings of intense vulnerability once she allowed herself to care, all surfaced now in relation to me. This was particularly exacerbated when I suffered a ski injury and was on crutches for an extended period. Acknowledging these feelings, however, allowed her to realize the ways in which she was not helpless and could survive disappointment.

Later, when things were going well with her boyfriend and she began to be increasingly able to enjoy sex and to experience orgasm, she expressed new fears that continued treatment, which had become the metaphor of her right to be her own person, might pose a threat to her love relationship. She was aware of impulses to resort to earlier patterns of sacrificing her own needs to avoid any risks. At the same time she expressed fears that she could not sustain the love relationship without treatment, fears that treatment would go on forever, and awareness of her resentment of her sense of dependence on me. As she articulated all of this, however, she was able to express how she felt stronger, more whole, and more independent than she had ever felt in her life.

She reported a vivid dream in which she was *"ostensibly dead, a marionette with invisible strings: The energy was in the strings. It takes a tremendous amount of concentration and energy to act dead. Someone came along and both saw and cut the strings. Suddenly the energy returned inside and I was forced to be awake. I am sure the someone was you."* Her associations were as follows: *"It was much easier when I had the strings. But I don't want to walk around faking and not know what's real or not. I can't fool myself anymore. Now I have to take responsibility. But being conscious can be horrifying. I feel very vulnerable."*

Dani elaborated that she felt as though she had been *"frozen for years and years in order not to feel pain"* and that now she was *"thawing."* She described the pain she felt now as *"almost unbearable"* and yet said that she felt more hopeful and more whole than she ever had before. In this context she reported a dream of *"frogs and turtles coming out of a pond where I thought there had been no life. That is what is happening with me. I am finding all these new things I didn't think were there. I am having all these little births."* She said she felt herself *"coming alive, being born,"* and that *"for the first time I am afraid of death because I feel alive."*

Clearly, risking this degree of vulnerability was not a simple matter, and the work that followed was no less tumultuous. Nevertheless, I believe this was a crucial moment in her life and in our work.

Later in Dani's treatment, after these changes had occurred, she was able to begin to describe with much emotion extremely painful and traumatic experiences in her childhood that she had never been able to talk about before.

I present this material from Dani's treatment to illustrate how this kind of process between patient and analyst can facilitate important internal changes in the patient and to emphasize the significance not only of the actual interaction between patient and analyst in such contexts as a medium for working through but also of being able to make this the focus of the work.

In my work with Dani—whose first dream in treatment was *"I was holding tubes of paint. If I were to drop them the world would explode like a nuclear reactor"*—the opportunity for her to discover that I was able to survive her manipulation, seduction and destructiveness, without rejecting her or becoming punitive, was extremely important. In addition, my holding her responsible and accountable for her behavior conveyed my belief that she was capable of being responsible at a time when she herself doubted her capabilities and provided an opportunity for her to discover resources in herself she had not realized she had. As she began to feel increasingly safe in relation to me and in relation to herself, and to understand by virtue of what actually occurred that there were possibilities between us and within herself she had not quite grasped before, she became willing to risk the kind of vulnerability that was integral to the awakening of desire.

This process with Dani shows us that even in the context of severe difficulties there are strivings for health and growth and that the capacity for new experience can be engaged. Learning how to help release these strivings poses an endless challenge. It also offers the promise of enabling us to refine our ways of working so as to be more effective with all patients, including those whose problems may be less extreme.

In the chapters following I will elaborate the technical considerations that informed the ways I used myself in this treatment, and the ways my work with Dani influenced the development of my own subsequent thinking about issues of technique. In this regard, I will try to illustrate how the kind of acute sensitivity to every nuance of the analyst's participation that becomes so clear with patients such as Dani alerts us to how profound the impact of the most subtle nuances of our participation as analysts is with all patients. It also helps to sensitize us to the degree to which the actual interaction between patient and analyst is often the locus of therapeutic action and the key to the question of analyzability in all contexts, including those in which it might be much less obvious how this might be so.

CHAPTER 2

Analytic Interaction
Beyond Words

ANALYSTS HAVE ALWAYS BEEN sensitive to the fact that the manifest content of what patients talk about is only the "tip of the iceberg." They are trained to look for hidden meanings and for latent content. What they have not always fully appreciated is the power of what goes on affectively between patient and analyst, the power of unconscious communication, and the degree of enactment and unconscious collusion that inevitably occurs in the analytic situation.

The fact that these interactive considerations have generally not been attended to is especially noteworthy given that as early as 1915 Freud wrote, "It is a very remarkable thing that the *Ucs.* of one human being can react upon that of another, without passing through the *Cs.*" (1915b, p. 194), and that in the 1930s Sullivan (1953) emphasized that the experience of anxiety was communicated without any need for words. In a similar vein, Ferenczi (1933) emphasized how much is communicated by both patient and analyst nonverbally.

With the growing body of literature on primitive forms of communication, including projective identification, as well as the growing body of infant research data, the power of preverbal, affective, and unconscious forms of communication becomes even more apparent.

In this chapter I focus on the degree to which analysis is a complex interpersonal process that involves dimensions of relatedness and experience, as well as of affective communication and enactment, that are not encompassed in the explicit content of what is verbalized but are often the locus of the most profound therapeutic action. My view is that, as we increase our understanding of the analytic significance of these dimensions, which often are elusive and hard to grasp, we will be able to refine our theory of technique in important ways.

Recognizing the power of what goes on beyond words is of course as important in context of verbalization as it is in the context of its absence. I will begin by addressing the former.

It is well known that words can serve as barriers or bridges to communication, or as both simultaneously. Words can be used to conceal or reveal; they can be used in an attempt to evoke feelings or to elicit certain kinds of behavioral responses; they can be weapons, camouflage, cries for help, a means to test another, gifts, or even a way to put ideas and images into the mind of another. They can be used to seduce, amuse, amaze, charm, insult, penetrate, invade, betray, hurt, shock, deceive, distract, manipulate. Being able to truly express oneself in words is a rare and special gift, and yet there are times when even with such a gift words are inadequate. Any effort to capture live experience, for example, is doomed to fall short of the mark, precisely because the very process of attempting to articulate it changes it so that what was true as one began to describe it is no longer true as one does so. Since words can be a medium for acting out by patient or analyst, and since what goes on affectively, often nonverbally, can have profound impact, both positive and negative, the importance of becoming more aware of the impact of what goes on beyond words, even in the context of verbal communication, cannot be overestimated.

An incident comes to mind:

A friend, who had been living with a woman for some time, one day reported that they had had a terrible fight. She asked him to move out. He packed his things and left. She became furious. He stated that he didn't understand why.

One can wonder whether her intent in asking him to leave was not to get him to leave but to test him or to hurt him. Or, did she think she wanted him to leave only to find out she did not? The fact that he not only did not seem hurt but in fact seemed to seize the opportunity to leave without a protest was apparently devastating to her. Who had initiated what? Had she been set up in some way she was not even aware of? Or had he? Had he been looking for an excuse to leave? Or was he too proud to stay under the circumstances? What is clear is that the subtleties of the scenario being enacted were not explicit in the verbal dialogue. The analytic relationship is equally, if not more, complex.

For example, in the analytic context taking a patient at his or her word when he or she says "I want to quit" may totally miss the point. It may actually constitute a devastating rejection, a lack of understanding, and/or an analytic abandonment.

Even when analyst and patient seem to be in agreement, it may well be that what is being enacted is a form of capitulation, submission, compliance, or a need to believe or to idealize what the other says. Or it may express sensitivity to the other's need on the part of either patient or analyst, or both.

One patient responded to something I had said by saying, *"I am sorry to disagree with you but . . . "*

When I asked if he was really sorry and noted that in fact he had seemed disappointed and perhaps even angry that I had not understood him immediately, his response was to document his own sense of himself as a "fraud." Though we could wonder whether he was thus complying again, he was able to articulate that his effort to always be conciliatory was a reaction to his fears of his own potential for violence. This became the basis for a productive exploration of very painful material.

Any interaction can involve self-mystification and/or symbolic enactment of some elaborate fantasy, conscious or unconscious, on the part of either or both participants. Even when the explicit dialogue is valid in its own terms, it can serve as a defense against dealing with other issues or aspects of the experience that might be more threatening to either or both participants, and may thereby reflect collusive enactment at another level. Free association, for example, can be used in the service of avoiding the analytic intimacy of the immediate moment, as a way to get oneself out of the room or to bring other people into the room, so that one does not have to be alone with the analyst. Alternatively, patients may engage in free association in response to some perception of the analyst's needs or fears of a more intimate engagement.

No matter how we conceptualize what is occurring, there is always another prism through which it can be viewed, always another level of abstraction. What becomes evident is the need to be sensitive to what is being enacted, even as it is also clear that any effort to address what is being enacted constitutes another level of potential enactment, often as complex as the interaction it presumes to illuminate.

Consider a situation in which a patient presents threatening material. To the extent that this evokes the analyst's sense of vulnerability, the analyst may be submitting to or colluding with the patient's hidden agenda without even being aware of it. If the analyst is able to address these interactive subtleties, even if after the fact, this not only helps illuminate what has occurred but also constitutes an assertion of analytic strength which has an impact itself.

A scenario comes to mind in which a patient suddenly withdraws or becomes remote or even hostile. Then the patient apologizes for this behavior. If the analyst takes this at face value, the interactive subtleties may never come to light. In addition, the analyst may be participating in a form of collusion with the patient's own self-mystification. In contrast, if the analyst is attentive to the fact that the patient's reaction may be in response to some interactive event, however subtle, and attempts to explore what this might have been, he or she may find that the patient was responding to some experience of injury by the analyst. In some instances, patients have responded this way when I have looked at the clock or made some facial expression of which I myself was unaware. In these instances, neither they nor I would have realized this was the case had I not made a point of pursuing the interactive subtleties. An even more sensitive exploration would require attending to what the analyst was reacting to when he or she looked at the clock or when his or her expression changed. My point simply is to suggest the degree to which recognizing the power of interactive forces, as they operate in both directions, often out of awareness, and in an ongoing spiral of reciprocity, can become an important way of expanding the analytic exploration.

Hearing the patient, as distinct from the patient's words, does not require knowing what is beyond the words, so much as recognizing that something is not being acknowledged or addressed. In this regard it is common knowledge that if the patient seems disconnected from his or her own experience, being able to address this explicitly can be quite useful. At times this can take the form of simply asking patients to stop talking so much or to stop thinking or working so hard, so as to be aware of what they may be feeling at any given moment. Even if the answer is "I do not know," this can be an important realization.

The power of what can be communicated without words was brought home to me with one particular patient.

PAULA

Paula, a woman in her late twenties, began treatment on a three-times-a-week basis eight months after her baby was born. She was suffering from a severe postpartum depression.

In the early period of our work she would often arrive late for her sessions and leave early, sometimes after only a few minutes. Sometimes she wouldn't show up at all. When she did come she was often unable to verbalize anything at all and was not able to sit still in the consulting room. On some occasions she would pace back and forth in an agitated way.

Once she began banging on and kicking the doors to my office. Although I was well aware of the potential for violence (she was in fact physically larger and stronger than I), I found myself more moved by her distress than frightened by her behavior. It seemed at that moment as though she felt somewhat like a wild animal captive in a cage, even as she seemed to be trying to convey to me how menacing she could be. I viewed this as important data, in that there are patients with whom I have felt more afraid with less apparent provocation. I commented that I sensed how terrified *she* seemed to feel. Her response was dramatic. It was as though the tigress suddenly turned to a kitten, as her eyes began to twinkle and she calmed down and became accessible in a way she had not been before.

As we continued to meet, though there was still not much verbalization, there began to be a great deal of direct eye contact between us. This would go on for long periods, during which neither of us looked away. If the buzzer rang, even though nothing was being said, it felt like an intrusive interruption. This only heightened our awareness of the growing intensity of our relationship and the increasingly intimate nature of our mutual silence. She was so shaken by such interruptions that when they occurred she might remark that "the spell was broken" and she had to leave.

Although she tended to come late and leave early when she did come, if by chance she was early or just on time and I was a few minutes late, she would leave. I quickly learned how careful I had to be in terms of her sensitivities and how fragile our connection felt, even for all its intensity. When she did not come to her sessions, she worried the connection between us would disappear or that it would turn out to have been illusory.

What became striking to me was the recognition of how much less charged and more "tame" were my relationships with some other patients, and the contrast between the fullness and intimacy of the silence with Paula and the emotional emptiness despite a profusion of words in some other situations. With her it felt as though there was nothing, not even words between us. If I were depressed, tired, upset, or feeling good, she knew in an instant. I could read her with the same accuracy in the same way.

Ultimately words did begin to enter our dialogue. Gradually she was able to describe her fears of her own violence and pathology, her fears of harming her child. She told of dreams filled with violence, often extremely gory. She also expressed her wish for me to know what she was experiencing without her having to tell me. As time went on she was able to articulate her fear that, were she to put things into words, parts of herself would "leak" out and slip away under the door, like a puddle, dispersing beyond any possibility of retention, cohesion, or recognition. Verbalizing this fear provided the opportunity for her to discover that she (and I) could survive such verbalization.

In this treatment the verbal dialogue seemed to become possible as a result of the powerful affective connection we were able to achieve, rather than the reverse, and I learned much from Paula about the significance of aspects of our interaction I would not have otherwise appreciated. (See Chapter 8 for details of a later period of our work together.)

The analyst not only hears beyond words but also communicates beyond words. Maldonado (1987), citing Lacan's conception of "full" and "empty" word (1953), emphasizes that when the patient is inauthentic, if the analyst relates to the "empty" word as though it were "full," or does not attempt to identify it as such and lets it go unremarked, the analyst is involved in a collusion that constitutes an interactive impasse. Little (1951) writes that the reverse is true as well: If the analyst is inauthentic and the patient colludes, this also constitutes an analytic impasse.

Whether the analyst is involved or indifferent, clinical in his or her demeanor or personally related, compassionate and tender or harsh and careless, patronizing or respectful, authentic or inauthentic, has an effect independent of the words spoken. Similarly, how we phrase and frame what we say places us in a very specific relation to the patient, which has an impact as well. The analyst's unconscious fears and fantasies also have significance, so that at times what we see in the patient may be a response to aspects of our own participation of which we may have no conscious awareness (Searles, 1990). If all of these interactive subtleties are not recognized, a vital part of the analytic dialogue is left unexplored and an opportunity for expanding the analytic intimacy is lost.

I have found that there are few things more important than attending to the effect of what I might have communicated without awareness or intention and to the fact that what I think I am communicating may be quite different from what the patient experiences. For example, one time I became so angry at a patient that I assumed it would no longer be possible for me to work with her. I was amazed when the patient reported how much it meant to her to know that I, too, could "lose it." For once she felt that she "was not the only bad one in the room." This interaction thus seemed to have had therapeutic impact and to have been valuable in ways I could never have consciously anticipated.

Similarly, at moments when I have found myself tearful in response to what a patient may have said or appeared unable to allow himself or herself to feel, my responsiveness, which was clearly uncalculated and spontaneous (and which at times I felt almost embarrassed about), seemed to release something in the patient, allowing her or him to experience feelings never allowed into consciousness before. At other times my responsive laughter has been catalytic (see Ehrenberg, 1984a, 1990), as patients have reported that discovering that I really enjoyed being with them affected them deeply. Some patients have reported that the opportunity to simply waste time, without evoking my condemnation, was extremely meaningful to them. One patient noted that my "casualness" and playfulness, as well as the fact I was not distant or aloof, were most important for him and made it possible for him to stay in treatment.

For many patients, finding that they can have an emotional impact on the analyst, positive or negative, or that the analyst is interested in knowing them may be what matters most. For some it is the opportunity to experience a nondestructive form of intimacy. For some the freedom to share aspects of their internal life that not even a sexual partner or spouse is privy to can be extremely meaningful.

One patient, Neil, helped focus the significance of several aspects of our interaction which I would not have appreciated otherwise.

NEIL

Neil, with whom I would meet four hours each week, would alternate between couch and chair depending on his own felt need. He reported that this enabled him to reach levels of emotion never experienced in a prior analysis. He stated that my letting him proceed in his own way convinced him that I was able to handle the intensity of his feelings, both positive and negative, and also allowed him to take risks he would not have dared to otherwise. Reflecting on our work, he reported, *"Something inside got repaired. When I would go into deeper hateful things on the couch, and when I would then go back and sit in the chair, there was definitely the feeling that for all the violence, the images of killing you and cutting you up, I hadn't lost you because of that."*

He stated through tears that my emotional presence and my commitment to standing by him as he struggled with frightening emotions had been critical in enabling him to reach important insights and make significant connections himself. He stated that my ability to stay with him where he "was," neither ahead nor behind, without trying to interpret what he was going through, let him know himself *"from the inside, not from the outside."*

He also felt it conveyed my trust in him and the fact that I didn't have to be in control or to "know," which meant a great deal to him precisely because mother and grandmother so often had to be in control and had to "know."

Later in treatment he described the joy he felt in realizing he could make me laugh. It was evidence that he was able to create feelings in me. *"The closest I have come to touching you is making you laugh."* He reported feeling so excited by the realization that he could thus actually cause my body to *"move and shake,"* and by the fact that we were able to talk so openly about all that was going on between us, that he wanted to cry.

About two years later, there was a period in which I would sometimes become drowsy in his sessions as he lay on the couch, to the point where I wondered whether I was avoiding something. In one session he asked whether I was awake. At that point I said that I was, but acknowledged that I was feeling somewhat "foggy." He reported, to my surprise, that the fact I could let him have that impact, and was not afraid to acknowledge it, was extremely meaningful to him. He felt it was indicative of the fact that I was willing to allow him to "affect" me in my body which, as before, touched him in a profound way. He elaborated that my response conveyed to him that I was not threatened by him and did not need to resist him and stand "outside." There were many associations to restful states of drowsiness next to his mother as she was nursing his sister, and how these were different from the states of tension and sense of danger he often felt between them otherwise. He noted of his experience now with me: *"This is rock bottom. It's important for me to experience that you can take me in on a psychological level and feel no need to reject my impact or to stand on the outside of that. That is why it's rock bottom. It answers the question, Am I lovable? It's even more basic, it answers whether it is it OK for me to be alive. It tells me that I am not foreign to you.*" There were complex and emotionally charged associations to his most fundamental fears about his own acceptability.

He later noted that in a prior analysis he was sure the analyst had similar drowsy experiences but that his former analyst would never admit it, and how important it had been to him that I had been willing to.

This example highlights how what goes on affectively and what is enacted, not necessarily with awareness, can advance the analytic process and can be the locus of profound kinds of therapeutic action. It also illustrates how recognizing and addressing this explicitly can increase the dimensions of the experience and expand the analytic dialogue.

Winnicott (1969, p. 86) has written, "It appalls me to think how much deep change I have prevented or delayed in patients *in a certain classification category* by my personal need to interpret."

An important consideration here is that "not interpreting" does not mean not responding. In this regard, I think it is essential to appreciate the degree to which the nature of the analyst's affective presence, availability, and openness to the experience constitute an important kind of responsiveness.

In this regard Winnicott has emphasized the "holding" function of the analytic relationship and its role as a facilitating environment, the potential for the analyst to be used as a transitional object, and the degree to which the opportunity to test the limits of one's own omnipotence and to discover that the analyst can survive the patient's "destruction" can be the most critical aspect of the analytic experience for some patients (Winnicott, 1951, 1963a, 1963b, 1969). He has also emphasized that there are times when we succeed by "failing," and that the value of an interpretation often lies in what it conveys about the limits of the analyst's understanding. Fromm-Reichmann (1950, 1952), Searles (1965), and Levenson (1972, 1983) have made similar points. Wolstein (1959), Singer (1971), and Searles (1975) have emphasized the therapeutic value for the patient of being able to feel useful, needed, appreciated by the analyst, or to be able to contribute to the analyst's growth. Racker (1957, 1968) and Bion (1967) have written about the analyst's role as "container."

Simply by maintaining an interested analytic presence the analyst may be providing a significant new experience for the patient.

In considering varying functions the analyst may serve, often without awareness, it is necessary also to recognize that at times the analytic relationship may be "triadic" rather than "dyadic," even though the analyst may not appreciate the degree to which this is so. Some analysts (Lacan, 1953; Mahler, 1967; Abelin, 1971, 1975; Mahler, Pine, and Bergman, 1975, and others) have focused on the role of the "father" (or the "third") in helping to free the child from the symbiotic relationship with the mother and in opening the door to certain kinds of symbolic capability. Where there has been some developmental failure in this regard, I think it is important to consider that the analyst may, often unwittingly, serve this kind of function (of being the "third").

For some patients, the fact that someone is willing to listen, interested in their experience, interested in knowing them, able to enjoy being with them, and willing to hang in there even when the going is rough, may have greater significance than any interpretation. At other times what may be most helpful may be the opportunity to discover that it is possible to engage in an intimate way without being violated or impinged on, without hurting or being hurt, or to just "be" as opposed to being faced with a demand to "work" in treatment.

Winnicott (1967, p. 115) described a patient whose analysis revolved around "'being seen' for what she in fact is, at any one moment; and at times the being actually seen in a subtle way is for her the main thing in her treatment."

Though insight in such contexts often comes as the result of "new experience" in the lived interaction, not from the analyst's interpretations, and often is the result of change rather than the cause of change, there are times when these interactions can lead to change without insight ever emerging. B. Ehrenberg (1980), for example, has observed that the experience with the analyst, often not consciously understood by either participant, can facilitate varying forms of "repair of the unconscious."

If such interactive subtleties are not recognized and addressed, a vital part of the analytic interaction is left unexplored and an opportunity for expanding the analytic intimacy is lost. On the other hand, if we are attentive to this dimension of the work and attempt to explicate it, we expand the analytic possibilities in important ways (Ehrenberg, 1974).

The following clinical example illustrates some ways of working that take these concerns into account. The emphasis is on structuring a process that opens the moment and allows for exploring it in all its richness and complexity and that enables the patient to begin to discover and utilize resources in himself or herself of which he or she may never have been aware. The premise is that ultimately this is what is most healing and liberating for the patient.

ELLEN

Ellen, an attractive professional woman in her thirties, began treatment on a twice-a-week basis. In a state of acute anxiety, Ellen was agitated and expressed fears she was having a "breakdown." She reported that she had just left a therapist she had been seeing for six years after he had begun to make sexual advances toward her. At first she felt flattered and pleased; only later did she begin to feel violated and betrayed. She said she had relied on him to advise her on "everything" up until then. She now felt angry and was aware that she had not changed in the ways she had hoped to after all those years. She stated that she was hesitant to trust another therapist and frightened by the power of her own seductiveness. She was clear that she wanted therapy and not analysis and that she wanted to work with a woman; in addition, she expressed fears that treatment could threaten her current marriage or precipitate a breakdown.

She was extremely verbal and articulate and had many ideas as to what her problems were and what she needed from me. Yet my impression, which I shared, was that everything that she verbalized seemed to be based on what she thought she *should* be feeling, wanting, needing, rather than on what she actually felt. She seemed surprised and interested as she acknowledged that this was in fact true and expressed her fear of touching her own experience and finding out about herself. She worried she might lose control were she to open herself to her own impulses.

In the sessions following she elaborated how angry she became when people were not able to give her what she needed, even when they couldn't, and how scared she felt. She described what a "good girl" she was with her former therapist and wondered how much of what she did in those years of treatment was for him or for herself, and whether she would regress without him.

There were also associations to how she had idealized her father, her first husband, and her former therapist, only later to realize that all of them were "crazy" and to leave them. She described feeling *"very weak and frightened realizing my gods were crazy. I feel a need to pull for myself. I don't want to build another god, but I don't know if I have the strength not to."*

What was striking was that, even as she verbally expressed her desire to not get into the same pattern of relying on me, my experience was that she seemed to be trying to maneuver me into being her advisor, asking me to make decisions for her and trying to elicit my approval.

As I focused on the discrepancy between what she said she wanted and what she seemed actually to be structuring in our interaction, we were able to clarify several things. First, there was her wish to be taken care of and not to be faced with having to make choices or take responsibility for herself. This included a wish for me to provide magical solutions for her, to guide her and tell her what to do, and a feeling of anger and betrayal when I did not. Second, there was her contempt for women in general, and me in particular. Her assumption was that the reason I did not offer answers and guidance was because I was a woman and didn't know how. Third, we uncovered the extent of her self-doubt and self-contempt. Fourth was the degree to which her seeming overt dependence and deference actually served as a way of remaining encapsulated and inaccessible, thereby protecting her from having to engage either the other (in this case the analyst) or herself. It became clear that this had been a way to remain in "control" and to prevent relationships from ever being psychologically "consummated."

As all this became clarified she produced a wealth of affectively charged associations and reported many dreams. We were able to clarify a fantasy that if she were to "submit," the other was to "provide." What she wanted from others was "protection, security and a feeling of identity." If they didn't provide this, she got angry, feeling that they were not fulfilling their part of the "deal."

Her reaction to my unwillingness to play by her rules and collude with her, even as she denied that this was what she wanted, was a combination of rage and fear. She cried as she revealed how inadequate she had felt all her life and how terrified she was to explore the limits of her own capability. Nevertheless, she began to surprise herself with the richness of her own associations and with her own insightfulness in response to her own material. In this context she began to cry and commented, *"I don't understand why all this comes out here. It must be something you are emoting to me. You are not saying very much, yet I feel an empathic quality that is hooking in and makes me feel safe and I can pour."*

This was particularly interesting, since even as she was giving me credit for being empathic she was negating the value of the things I had said and of the fact that my silences had been as deliberate as my verbal interventions. Clarifying her efforts to minimize my role elicited associations to how competitive she felt towards me and how intensely she needed to devalue me.

She reported a strong fear of getting close and then being left, said she felt much more comfortable being close to a man than to a woman, and expressed her fear that if she got close to me I might leave her or have a breakdown as her mother had had. She felt that the effort to devalue me was at least in part a way to protect herself from this kind of threat.

There was much emotion relating to both the content of this realization and to her realization of her own contribution to piecing this together. She stated, *"I feel what is happening here is good, yet I don't understand why I can't give you or myself any credit. If you were a man I would be walking around saying I found the greatest therapist. But since it's you it only feels like meeting for lunch. It's like a relationship that is empty. But it is working and I can't understand it. (Crying) I don't understand how I talk the way I do here. I almost feel brighter and more reflective than I ever thought."*

I asked her why this seemed so painful. She replied, *"I feel like I am in a dilemma, at a crossroads. Like I have to give up something (now sobbing); it's been punctured. Like I have to give up my father. I never had sessions like this. I never knew I had the capacity to think or feel like I do here."*

There were many associations to her relationship with her father.

In the session following (the sixteenth), she reported that she was feeling better and no longer worried about having a breakdown. She noted that she was pleased she was not idealizing me as she had her former therapist. She stated that a question I had raised the session before about how much of her feelings were based on a fantasy person rather than on the real person had really hit home.

Then she casually noted that I looked different when she had her glasses on from when she did not. She added that she preferred the way I looked without her glasses, saying that without them I looked "younger and softer," and with them I looked "harder and older." She proceeded to take them off.

Intrigued, I noted that, although she had said she was glad she was not "idealizing" me, she then described how she was choosing to see me as she preferred.

This seemed to strike a chord, and she responded with associations to her relationship with her father and to the fact that she had always tended to idealize him, to see him as "the greatest man in the world." She described the pain — and then rage — she experienced when she finally *saw* him as he really was, and said that this had been true with her former husband and her former therapist as well.

At that point she began to sob and stated that this experience of being confronted with how she was *choosing* to see me as she preferred was the first time she was aware of "twisting reality" to meet her image of what she wanted to see: *"I knew I was manipulative, I knew I idealize, but I never knew I was doing that with reality."*

She then put on her glasses but looked away from me, stating, *"I don't feel like looking at you. Then I don't have to make a choice."*

There was more material about how she had not allowed herself to "see" throughout her life. She sobbed as she stated, *"How come I never saw that that was what I was doing?"*

This was followed by expressions of ambivalence toward me, as well as resentment that I had been instrumental in helping her to "see" all of this. There were also additional associations to her father. She elaborated how he devalued women and how she idealized him, yet on some level *saw* what he was doing. She described his contempt for women, his hypocrisy, how badly he had treated her mother and how angry she currently felt towards him. And as she began to elaborate what she viewed to be the sordid details of his past, she described feeling as though she were betraying him and fearing his retribution even from his grave. She further detailed how painful and conflicted their relationship had been, the fights that went on in her adolescence, and her terror of his rages. She now stated that she didn't know *"how much of the good memories were reality, and how much were fabrications of what I wanted to believe."*

She added, *"I feel like you are giving me a chance to come to all this on my own. It's painful but it's better."*

In the eighteenth session she reported that she was agitated and anxious. She had had a dream in which, *"We were on your couch together. We were under a blanket tickling toes. You stroked my arm as though to say I should talk. Another girl, eighteen years old, walked in. She was me. She was very pretty. It was as though I was being outshined by my younger self. I woke up very scared."*

Her associations were that she felt she was getting close to me; that was scary and she was angry it was happening. *"I realize that the only way I was able to survive was by seeing my mother as a nonentity, being contemptuous of her. I wish I could put you down, or desexualize you, say you are 'dykey,' but I can't. Then I have to struggle with all the feelings about the mother I didn't have. I realize I am looking for something I was missing. It's terrifying. It makes me angry."*

There were associations to her younger self in the dream. She said she realized she is not as pretty now as she used to be when she was younger and that this scares her. Before she never felt there was any competition. She began to cry and continued, *"If I do get close to you, what is going to happen to me? It's so scary. Why can't I defend against it better? (Still crying) Are you going to be able to help me get through this? I never had this kind of therapy."*

Two sessions later (session twenty), she revealed the extent of her phobias and of her anxieties in a way she had not done before. These included fears of heights, of enclosed spaces, of elevators, of swimming, of animals, of bike riding, of the ocean, and of leaving New York City. When she was faced with any of these things, her legs became paralyzed, she sweated, and she had palpitations. She had avoided all of these things for as long as she could remember. This was followed in the subsequent session by a statement: *"I realize my terror is as intense as my mother's. I realize I am just like my mother."*

She began to sob and to wonder why she had never been able to "see" this before. *"How can this be happening? How come no one ever told me how connected I am to her? If you had said anything it would have blocked me. God damn Freud with his unconscious! It's so unbelievable that I outsmarted myself like this. This is probably why I never went into 'analysis.'"*

In the session following she reported that *"last session was unbelievable. It was a breakthrough; it was as though something came crashing down. The truth became clear, like the pieces of a puzzle fit together. I felt an incredible sense of relief from anxiety and terror. I was able to write a paper without my usual anxiety and terror, I was able to do exercises at the gym that I never would have tried before, I had my eyebrows tweezed and didn't go through my usual terror . . . and I was able to talk to my mother normally for the first time."*

Nevertheless there was also a sense that she had been *"outsmarted. . . . I got caught and the secret came out."* She elaborated that she had been thinking about her relationships, her ambivalence and anxieties in relation to me, about wearing or not wearing her glasses and what that meant. *"I am exhilarated about all of this and very hopeful, and I am very scared. (Cries) But I don't feel terror and anxiety."*

There were associations to the ways in which she realized she had come between her parents at certain times, which she related to her current fears about having a child. She wondered whether her fear was that a child might interfere with her marriage. There were associations to her sense that her father had always preferred her to her mother and had been quite overt about this.

She then revealed how intense her feelings toward me were becoming. She also expressed a fear that I might want to have a sexual relationship with her.

At that point I noted that she seemed to feel that, in order to be close to me or to anyone she had to put herself at the mercy of the other. She began to sob and nodded "yes," stating, *"As a kid I would do almost anything so as not to be left alone. My fantasy was that I had to yield totally."*

There were associations to her mother, to her mother's unavailability, and to her own feelings of frustrated longing and desperate loneliness. There were also associations to her father, how she wanted to be his girlfriend, become his confidante, and his intellectual companion, but how the only way to be with him was on his terms.

By session twenty-four she noted that she felt close to me and vulnerable, but felt tricked into it. *"It happened without my seeing it coming."*

She expressed fears I might turn on her, yet said she was glad I was her "analyst." (She had originally emphasized that she did not want analysis.) She added, however, that she was sad about this too, because, *"Now I can never experience you as a friend. You are probably someone I would like to know. I don't understand why I feel so comfortable with you."*

In the following session (twenty-five) she reported, *"I feel depressed and angry. I can't put my finger on what I am upset about. I don't like to believe it has anything to do with you."*

When I inquired about this she stated, *"I felt Monday I was making myself vulnerable. Something started to get uncovered about my inability to get close without losing myself. Maybe it was too much for me to deal with. (Cries) I don't understand what goes on here so that I cry. I feel a weakening inside, and yet you keep emphasizing the boundaries, which is what I pay you to do. I guess there must be something frustrating about that. I don't know what's going on. Yet I don't feel I am losing myself. I do feel separate. This is painful because I have to look at things I don't want to see. How come you don't talk?"*

(The statement "this is what I pay you to do" was interesting as a measure of a shift from the helpless compliant stance of the first sessions to an increasing sense of her own power and responsibility in our relationship.)

By the next session (twenty-six) she was able to express how powerful her reaction was to what she perceived to be my responsiveness to her. She stated, *"Last week when you looked at me it was uncanny. You were not a shade off. Your facial expression sort of* went right into my gut. *I remember as a little kid wanting to be close to my cousin. I was so desperate I was going to give her money to let me lie next to her. I developed a system of defenses. Now I am angry. How dare you penetrate my defenses! How dare you get that close! How dare you be able to affect me at all!"*

She continued, *"Now I worry about lesbian fantasies. I know you are becoming an integral part of my life."*

As she articulated all of this, the terror and anxiety she had expressed in earlier sessions that she might become the helpless victim of a seduction by me were relieved. She was able to acknowledge her fear of her own impulses and how turned on she was by her own fantasy of "yielding totally." Her response to all of this was to note that now, for the first time, she had some hope that maybe it was possible not to have to *"live this way forever."*

Two sessions later she reported two dreams. In the first a friend said to her: *"The reason I couldn't get along with you is that you perform."* In the second she related, *"I interviewed a female therapist who did not have time to see me. Then I interviewed a male and found him ineffectual. I went back to the woman and insisted she must see me and the woman finally agreed. I was impressed with my own effectiveness. It was noticeably out of character, something new for me."*

There were associations to early relationships in which she never dared to "be" herself, and how she always performed, relating to others on what she imagined to be their "terms."

At this point she stated that her reaction to these two dreams was the "realization" that she wanted to start analysis with me: *"You win. I have decided to start analysis with you. I realize something is happening internally. I am not feeling as devaluing or angry. It isn't just toward you. It is also toward myself. I also feel less contemptuous of my mother. For the first time in my life I am not anxious. Instead I am excited and curious about what is going to happen. I feel stronger. I was able to go down a spiral staircase. My husband couldn't believe it. I used to be phobic about it. I realize I never took a look at myself before and I don't know what I am going to find. But I know I want to and I want to do it with you."*

Obviously, her initial statement "you win" was quite complex, and had to be explored, given our earlier discussions of the erotiza-

tion of what it meant to "yield" to another, as well as her history of
being the compliant patient. Nevertheless, this proved to be the
beginning of a very productive analysis that went on for several
years.

One of the things I have tried to show is that analytic work is best
advanced by facilitating a process in which the patient, not the
analyst, is the one to arrive at the major insights on his or her own,
and in which the patient has the opportunity to discover resources
in himself or herself of which he or she had been unaware. Such
experiences are strengthening, contribute to an increasing sense of
confidence both in the treatment and in oneself, and can lead to
increased hopefulness and willingness to risk. Sensitivity to the
importance of what goes on beyond words is often essential to
facilitating this kind of achievement.

CHAPTER 3

The "Intimate Edge"

ATTENDING TO THE MOST SUBTLE aspects of what goes on *interactively* in the analytic relationship, in an almost microanalytic way, increases the dimensions of the immediate experience and actually transforms it, generating a unique trajectory of evolving experience at what in effect becomes the "intimate edge" of the relationship (Ehrenberg, 1974).

Focusing on the interface of the analyst-patient interaction is not the same as focusing on the patient or the analyst. Rather, it is the nature of the integration, the quality of contact, what goes on between, including what is enacted and what is communicated affectively and/or unconsciously, that is addressed.

The "intimate edge" ideally becomes the *point of maximum and acknowledged contact at any given moment in a relationship without fusion, without violation of the separateness and integrity of each participant.* Attempting to relate at this point requires ceaseless sensitivity to inner changes in oneself and in the other, as well as to changes at the interface of the interaction as these occur in the context of the spiral of reciprocal impact. This kind of effort, in itself, tends to have reflexive impact on both participants, and this in turn influences what then goes on between them in a dialectical way.

The "intimate edge" thus is never static but becomes the trace of a constantly moving locus. Each time this is identified it is also changed, and as it is reidentified it changes again. The analytic expanse is enlarged significantly as aspects of the relationship that are generally not explicitly acknowledged or addressed, as well as their vicissitudes over time, are identified and explored in an analytic way. The emphasis is on process, on engaging live experience, and on generating a new kind of live experience by so doing, in an ever expanding way.

In some ways the focus is on what Winnicott (1971) refers to as the "continuity-contiguity moment" in relatedness. What distinguishes my conceptualization is the *necessity for acknowledgment and explicitness,* since I believe the process of acknowledgment increases the moment's dimensions and changes the nature of one's experiences of it. What is achieved is not simply greater insight into what is or was, but a new kind of experience.

Working at the "intimate edge" creates a unique context of safety and allows for maximum closeness precisely because it protects against the threat of intrusion or violation. Attending to the most elusive interactive subtleties and "opening the moment" actually becomes a way to detoxify the field, as dangers of mystification, seduction, coercion, manipulation, or collusion are minimized (Levenson, 1972, 1983; Ehrenberg 1974, 1982a; Feiner, 1979, 1983; Gill, 1982b, 1983; Hoffman, 1983). In some instances this makes it possible for both participants to engage aspects of experience and pathology that otherwise might be threatening, even dangerous.[5]

The protection of the kind of analytic rigor that attending to interactive subtleties provides allows for more intense levels of affective engagement without the kind of risk this might otherwise entail.

In effect, the "intimate edge" is not simply at the boundary between self and other, the point of developing interpersonal intimacy and awareness of interpersonal possibility in the relationship; it is also at the boundary of self-awareness. It is a point of expanding self-discovery, at which one can become more "intimate" with one's own experience through the evolving relationship with the other, and then more intimate with the other as one becomes more attuned to oneself. Because of this kind of dialectical interplay, the "intimate edge" becomes the "growing edge" of the relationship.

As moment-by-moment shifts in the quality of relatedness and experience between analyst and patient are studied, individual patterns of reaction and particular sensitivities can be identified and explored. This allows for awareness of choices, as decisions to become increasingly involved, or to withdraw, as well as the influences these may be responsive to, can be studied in process, and the feelings surrounding these can be examined. The patient's spontaneous associations to the immediate experience often not only become an avenue to affectively charged memories of past experiences that might not have been previously accessible but also allow for the metaphoric articulation of unconscious hopes, fears, and expectations.

Even when the "intimate edge" is missed and there is some kind of intrusion or some failure to meet due to overcautiousness, the *process* of aiming for it, the mutual focus on the difficulties involved, can facilitate its achievement. The effort to study the qualities of mutual experience in a relationship, the interlocking of both participants, including a mutual focus on the failure to connect or on inauthenticity or collusion, can thus become the bridge to a more intimate encounter.

The "intimate edge" is, therefore, not a given, but an interactive creation. It is always unique to the moment and to the sensibilities of the specific participants in relation to each other and reflects the participants' subjective sense of what is most crucial or compelling about their interaction at that moment.

Focusing on the interactive nuances in this way often requires a shift in perspective as to what is figure and what is ground. For example, where a patient drifts into a fantasy that figuratively takes him or her out of the room, the interactive meaning is as important as the actual content (if not more so). Exploring what triggered the fantasy, and what its immediate interactive function might be, may help the patient grasp some of the subtler patterns of his or her own experience. While the content of the fantasy can provide useful clues to its function, staying with content may be a way for both patient and analyst to collude in avoiding engaging the anxieties of the moment.

Where some form of collusion does occur, as at times it inevitably will, demystifying the collusion has internal repercussions as well. The clarification of patterns of self-mystification (Laing, 1965) that this makes possible is often liberating. It can facilitate a shift on the part of the patient from feeling victimized or helpless, stuck without any options, to freshly experiencing his or her own power and responsibility in relation to multiple choices.

For example, one patient who had difficulty defining where she ended and the other began was invariably in a constant state of anger with others for what she perceived as their not allowing her her feelings. As we explored how this operated between us, she realized that no one could control her feelings and that it was her own inordinate need for the approval of others that was controlling her. It was her need to control the other, to control the other's reaction to her, that was defining her experience. The result was that she began to feel less threatened and paranoid. She also was able to begin to deal analytically with the unconscious dynamics of her needs for approval and for control, and to focus on her anxieties in a way not possible earlier.

Particularly where a patient might become "aware" so as to comply with what he or she believes the analyst considers necessary or desirable, the demystification of the interactive subtleties can be pivotal. It can evoke emotionally charged associations to the past and the recovery of important memories.

Aiming for the "intimate edge" requires that the analyst be acutely sensitive to inner changes, as well as to changes at the interface of the interaction, as these occur in the context of the spiral of reciprocal impact. Because of this the analyst must be able at times to work from *within* the countertransference. Even if we ourselves don't know why we are responding at a given moment, we can still use our reaction as a clue to the fact that something in the interaction may need to be clarified and addressed. (I will elaborate on this in later chapters.) The analyst's affective sensitivity is particularly key where the patient may not be fully in touch with this dimension of his or her own experience. If the analyst can use his or her own experience when the patient cannot, this can help to locate the affective center of experience in the immediate moment. When this occurs, it can be like opening a mine shaft leading into the depths of an emotional core.

On the other hand, where there may be a countertransference problem, aiming for the intimate edge may help to locate it even if the analyst is not aware. For example, a supervisee related that a patient he had recently begun to see was reporting self-destructive behavior outside of treatment. The patient had never engaged in such behavior before. The analytic candidate was eager to arrive at some theoretical formulation based on this information and on historical data he had gathered, so that he could make some interpretative intervention. I suggested that the student consider that the patient's report might have as much to do with the patient's relationship to the analyst and to the treatment as to anything else, and that he try to address what might be going on between them.

The following week the supervisee reported with excitement that when he tried to explore the patient's feelings about the treatment and about himself, the patient became extremely responsive and commented that he felt like crying. The patient was then able to articulate specific anxieties about the kind of attachment he believed he might want with the analyst. His fear was that the analyst would find this repellent, a fear he backed up with evidence based on the analyst's responses to him. He elaborated relevant reactions to experiences of partings and greetings with the analyst and of seeing the analyst with other patients who came before or after him. The analytic candidate had not been aware of these as having affected the patient.

In this instance, aiming for the intimate edge not only set the work back in motion but also enabled the patient to alert the supervisee to the fact that he (the supervisee) did have anxieties about a more intimate kind of engagement and about what this might portend given the intensity of the patient's feelings for him and the patient's evident neediness. The analytic field was significantly expanded as a result. (This kind of intervention, of course, often derives some of its power from the fact that it conveys to the patient that the analyst is no longer afraid to try to engage the moment, even if it is difficult.)

A similar shift in figure and ground is often useful where focusing on old concerns can be a way of avoiding engaging the present (by either or both participants). Attending to *why* something from the past is activated at particular moments, and how its use may be in response to what is going on in the immediate interaction, can become a way to move into present reality. This enlivens the experience and generates a new perspective and a new set of analytic and experiential possibilities. Ironically, clarifying either person's defensive use of the past may trigger an associative process that then opens onto the past with a new kind of emotional meaning.

Attending to the interactive subtleties in this way also helps sensitize us to the impact of how we position ourselves in relation to our patients. If we think we are being "collaborative" and find that the patient experiences our participation as authoritarian, or even patronizing, or interprets our behavior in other ways that we never would have been able to anticipate, this can help illuminate transference-countertransference issues that might otherwise elude us.

This kind of engagement also can help to clarify the analyst's limitations, thereby providing an opportunity for the patient to work through fears, fantasies, patterns of idealization, illusions and reactions to disillusion, even extreme degrees of punitiveness and intolerance, in an ongoing way. The confrontation with the complexities of reactions to disappointment can at times open the way to working though patterns of self-mystification. In some instances it leaves the door open for the patient's own creative gestures and for the development and recognition of resources of which he or she may have been unaware.

In aiming for the "intimate edge," the goal is not to transcend distance but to identify the distancing tendencies and to help illuminate how they affect what occurs. In this regard, Guntrip (1969, p. 105) described the "sense of a gulf which the patient cannot cross but which perhaps the therapist can and does if he shows the patient that he knows about it." He saw this as being of the highest importance in treatment. What I am emphasizing is the necessity to focus on this very gulf between. If the analyst tries to bridge such gulfs to form a more vital connection, an important analytic opportunity may be foreclosed, as the anxieties and distancing patterns themselves may be obscured rather than engaged.

In this vein Winnicott; (1965) has noted that there are healthy uses of noncommunication in the developing child. The development of the self many involve "a sophisticated game of hide and seek in which it is a joy to be hidden but a disaster not to be found" (p. 186). What I am stressing is that, to the extent this may be operative in the treatment context, working at the "intimate edge" requires clarifying that one makes choices about what to hide and what to seek. The ways in which these choices are made may be responsive to interactive subtleties, often out of awareness.

Paradoxically, engaging in the kind of exploration I am suggesting, which involves respecting personal boundaries and attempting to illuminate their significance and function, tends to open the way to greater intimacy. This is precisely how we turn a boundary into an "intimate edge." The opportunity this creates for the patient to experience in the immediate situation that a constructive kind of intimacy is indeed possible can be a revelation. On the other hand, an effort to press past boundaries most likely would preclude intimacy and might be experienced as a form of symbolic rape or violation.

The goal is to make it possible for anxieties, feelings, and fears about contact to be identified and addressed, rather than smoothed over and obscured. Where there is a pathological lack of boundaries, the same applies. We must help clarify that this is so, and in what ways. Staying clear and assuming a protective role so as to avoid intrusion without addressing the boundary issues does not allow the difficulties and vulnerabilities to be identified and engaged. In effect, an authentic encounter *can be facilitated* by acknowledging the limits of what may be possible at any given moment, where ignoring these or pretending these do not exist precludes a more genuine and penetrating kind of engagement (see Farber, 1966, and Maldonado, 1987, among others).

My emphasis on the importance of this kind of engagement is consistent with Buber's view that profound growth and change in the treatment situation occur in the context what he labeled an "I-Thou" relation, in contrast to an "I-It" relation. He called its unfolding the "dialogical" (1957b, p. 106). I believe the emphasis, as

Buber notes, is on *dialogue*. The dilemma, however, is how to facilitate this kind of dialogue. Aiming for the intimate edge seems to be
uniquely effective where this may be problematic.

   In a similar vein, Guntrip (1969) states that

> what is therapeutic when it is achieved is 'the moment of
> real meeting' of two persons as a new transforming experi-
> ence for one of them, which is, as Laing said (1965), 'Not
> what happened before [i.e. transference] but what has never
> happened before [i.e. a new experience of relationship].' (p.
> 353, bracketed additions in original)

He stresses that what is key is that analyst and patient meet
"mentally face to face" and come to "know each other as two human beings."

   I believe that at best such moments are transforming for analyst
as well as patient (see Buber's views 1957a, 1957b, 1958), and that
the opportunity to realize this can be influential in itself. Furthermore, my view is that Guntrip's "moment of real meeting" is not an
end, but is itself an important starting point that may have continuing leverage in the analytic process.

   *Analytic work does not stop when contact is made or when each
is truly touched in some profound way by the other and by their
interaction; rather, it takes on new dimensions as the affective complexity of what gets activated in the moments of meeting can be
clarified and explored in an endless progression.*

   When positive feelings develop, much is to be gained from an
exploration of how the patient understands why he or she feels
better, how he or she understands shifts between states of feeling
better and worse in general, and how he or she experiences the
impact of the analyst's participation. It can serve to clarify the
patient's awareness of or fantasies about these nuances of experience.

   As reactions to intimacy and distance, as well as fears and fantasies about moments of emotional contact (or lack of emotional
contact), are clarified, they can also be worked through in the immediate interaction. For some patients, the opportunity to discover
that neither participant need be damaged or diminished by the

experience or expression of positive feelings and closeness is as crucial as discovering that it is possible to survive negative ones. The discovery that it is possible to talk about such feelings with the person with whom one is experiencing them can also be significant. At times this kind of exploration at the intimate edge will expose a collusive need to maintain an idealized view of the analyst. This opens the way to dealing not only with feelings of disappointment and disillusionment, but also with tendencies toward compliance or even submission, among a multitude of possibilities. This process affirms the need for the patient take an active role in the work, while providing an opportunity for the patient to discover that he or she has something to offer (Singer, 1971; Wolstein, 1959, 1971).

Of course, the unique kind of intimacy this process structures has effects and consequences of its own and can itself become problematic. At times it can be experienced as seductive. This too can be grist for the mill. The point is that avoiding this kind of intimacy can preclude an analytic possibility altogether.

The perspective implicit in this orientation is different from those that have emphasized the importance of the "real relationship" between analyst and patient as a facilitating condition for successful analysis but do not see it as the actual medium of the analytic work. *Analytic work actually takes place within, and is a function of, the two-person interaction and of the new experience that is generated within it.* Aiming for the "intimate edge" is a way of extending the reach of psychoanalytic interaction.

Some clinical examples follow.

EDWARD

At one point in the course of his treatment, Edward spoke at length about how miserable he felt and how hopeless he believed he was. Despite the pain this might imply, it sounded to me like some kind of recording. It felt as though he were trying to put me off rather than communicating his feelings to me. I shared my reaction. He reflected on it and came up with the realization that he preferred to keep a distance between us. He formulated that what he had been involved in with me was actually a "pretense" of a relationship. I asked for his associations and he produced memories of experiences of humiliation as a child when he did allow others, particularly his mother, to get close to him.

When asked to elaborate, he said he did not see the point of all this but if it would make me "happy" he would try. I then asked what he meant by "if it would make you happy." He replied that he was willing to go along with my suggestion, even though it seemed a waste of time to him, to avoid a hassle and make things simpler for himself. He also stated that this was the way he usually "kept people off his back."

I suggested that trying to "humor" me certainly would not lead to my being able to help him with his problem. If anything it might preclude it. He replied that he did not think it was a "big deal." I commented that I thought it was and suggested that he consider this.

He then elaborated on some experiences with his mother that had been extremely painful. As he spoke about these experiences he began to show a degree of emotion he had never displayed before. I noted this and said that I felt moved as I listened. He indicated that he was surprised and touched by this and responded by elaborating with a great deal of feeling how lonely and isolated he felt.

Then, suddenly, he reverted to his former attitude, acting extremely indifferent and saying, *"What's the point of all this anyway, it's all hopeless."* I questioned the shift. He had no explanation and said it was not important anyway. I said I thought it was very important and suggested we try to figure out what might have triggered this sudden shift. As we examined what had just gone on between us in minute detail, I then realized that I had in fact glanced at the clock just prior to his shift in attitude. I mentioned this to him and wondered if he thought he might have reacted to my glancing away. At that point we were able to unravel a sequence in which I had looked at the clock as he was talking, he had experienced this as evidence of my lack of interest, felt hurt, and automatically pulled back.[6]

We both thus became exquisitely aware that his surface indifference masked a deep sensitivity and a great deal of feeling. At this point he began to cry. This was followed by an expression of his concern that I would experience his tearfulness as childish and weak. I indicated that, on the contrary, I saw his ability to be this open with me as a sign of courage and hopefulness. His response to this was one of surprise and "feeling good."

In the next session he was considerably more open than usual. He began to share some important details about his past and present life, details that he had been withholding. I found myself very conflicted. I was glad to learn all of this, and felt it was important to our work together that he had now decided to tell me; nevertheless, I noted that, although he had always questioned my trustworthiness in relation to him, I now felt troubled by the realization that he had been withholding so much from me. It made me wonder how trustworthy he was. He objected and said he had never actually lied; furthermore, he had been more honest with me than with anyone in his life. He hastened to assure me not to take it "personally."

I questioned his "reassurance," whereupon he said he was only trying to be "nice." I said I thought it would be better if he were honest. He became distressed and asked whether this meant I did not want to work with him anymore. I expressed my surprise at his question and at his expectation that that would be my reaction. I noted that, on the contrary, it now seemed we had a sounder basis for working together than before.

I also began to wonder out loud with him why was I reacting so strongly. I then began to consider that perhaps the issue was that I was upset with myself for not being more perceptive about the degree of his withholding. In response he expressed surprise that I should have any feelings about it at all and stated that he suddenly saw me as more "human" than before and that he now felt "more equal" than he ever imagined he could feel.

The work that followed included the exploration of feelings that had not been accessible before. It also provided an opportunity for him to gain a sense of his own maneuvers in the situation and served to highlight the issue of his responsibility in our relationship. Despite periods of doubt and ambivalence, as well as returns to his "affectless" posture, he began to speak of experiencing more "choices" and of feeling less helpless and to take a more active role in the work.

At another point in his treatment, as we focused on our immediate interaction and why at times it was so problematic, he was able to express intense fears that letting anyone come too close was to leave himself terrifyingly vulnerable. As we tried to determine how exactly this operated between us, he was able to articulate that he felt he could protect himself by not allowing himself to think about or to respond to any of my comments while he was with me. Instead he would think about them privately, away from me, and avoid any risk. In effect, he believed he could protect his private self by not bringing it to our sessions. Once this was explicit, it became possible to see that by doing this he was actually setting it up so that anything I said loomed very "large" in relation to his own feelings of "smallness" by virtue of his not really feeling present or having his own resources available to him while we were together. By absenting himself he actually felt he had no basis for accepting or rejecting anything I said; consequently, he felt vulnerable and frightened.

Uncovering this pattern revealed that it was he who actually kept himself vulnerable and defenseless. He began to consider that he didn't have to cut himself off from himself in order to cut himself off from me (or anyone else) if that was what he wanted, since no one could read his mind. It also allowed him to confront the possibility that he might have had other motives for cutting himself off from himself and to explore what these might be.

AMY

Amy, a young woman whose experience of herself was extremely fluid, was in a constant state of anxiety that she would lose herself or be overrun if she dared to be involved with anyone or anything outside herself. She described how she spent a great deal of time riding on trains because as long as she was in motion she believed she was in no danger of getting swallowed up or lost in any one place.

The only thing she could get involved with and enjoy was music, *"because music is temporary and ends and then I am out of it."* The same was obviously true for our sessions, which had a predefined beginning and end. Anything that required active disengagement felt threatening, in that she was not sure she would be able to manage this.

In her interactions in general she was expert at setting up triangles in which two people would argue over what she should do. So long as there were two people fighting over her she was safe from being influenced unduly by either one, as she played each off against the other to protect herself from both. All the while she felt she was simply an innocent bystander.

She had great difficulties in relationships where there was no third person involved. In such contexts she tended to feel that she was at the mercy of the other, unable to resist his or her influence and "control." She seemed to have no awareness of the degree to which she actually manipulated these situations so as to get the other person to make decisions for her. Her experience was that the other was trying to "control" her and she would feel angry about this.

Although we had made some slight headway with regard to her being able to recognize all of this, in one session, even as she spoke with some degree of awareness, she tried to set up an interaction in which I was to be the advocate of her taking responsibility for her own life and making her own decisions, while she would argue the case for not doing so. I pointed out that trying to structure this kind of debate between us was another example of what we had been talking about.

I observed that structuring her relationships in this way, by creating a sense of a conflict between herself and the other, seemed to allow her to avoid having to deal with some internal conflict. Furthermore, I told her it was not for me to tell her what to do: I could only help her to recognize her own conflict.

She responded by becoming silent. Then she acknowledged her awareness of this pattern. I remained silent. She then reported a dream which had been very upsetting. In the dream her leg had been shot and she was bleeding profusely, but since people around her seemed to ignore it, she did too. It was clear to her now that this was at risk to her own life. She was able to see the potential danger of trying to get other people to make decisions for her and of not taking responsibility for herself.

At the end of the session she tearfully expressed her feeling that this was important. The fact that I had let her struggle with it made her feel "listened to" and closer to me. However, at the same time it was extremely painful for her and she resented me because it made her feel separate and aware of the boundaries between us, which made her feel lonely and lost. She now elaborated that if I had argued with her or told her what to do, it would have permitted her to feel involved and connected. That would have been less difficult and painful for her than the state of separateness with which my not arguing confronted her. I replied that giving up that kind of illusion might allow for a more genuine connection. Her response was that a more genuine involvement would be frightening because it aroused her fears that she might "lose" herself, even as she herself noted that the dream had poignantly made clear to her that her line of defense was actually bringing about the state of affairs she most feared.

While this was not a totally new insight, the situation of having to confront the interactive pattern helped focus the issue and open it to analytic exploration, rather than allowing it to continue to be enacted in our relationship.

Sometime later in treatment she reported a dream in which people were walking through the walls in her apartment. This time she found the dream exciting. She elaborated that although the dream vividly articulated her fears, the fact that she had had such a dream affirmed her sense of self and of her own creative ability to produce such a dream.

Marcia

Marcia, a young woman who had great difficulty free associating or even lying on the couch without looking at me, began a session describing, with considerable anxiety, a sexual experience in which she could not distinguish between her body and her lover's.

As she focused on the physical aspects of this experience, I asked if she thought that the boundary problem might be psychological rather than physical. She angrily replied that I wasn't making sense and that I was confusing her. I acknowledged that I could see how my question might have been confusing. I noted, nevertheless, that I thought there might be value in our looking at her experience of confusion, rather than only looking at what I was doing that had confused her. (In this instance my sense was that focusing on the interaction might be a way of avoiding some important aspect of her own experience.) I also asked whether she thought that the confusion she was experiencing now was similar to what she had described experiencing with her boyfriend.

Despite her anger, this idea seemed to interest her, and she began to articulate a combination of feelings of disappointment, anger, anxiety and inadequacy. She acknowledged that it was her usual pattern to try to "get rid" of these feelings by focusing on the other and blaming that person for her distress. We were able to establish that by so doing she seemed to lose track of where she ended and the other began, as with her boyfriend. At the same time it became clear that if she saw others as responsible for her difficulties this made her feel helpless and dependent on them to "make her feel better."

At this point she was able to lie on the couch and not look at me. As she did so she came up with an image of having a field to cultivate, with no tools. She was able to describe the feelings of anxiety, inadequacy, and helplessness this evoked and her wish to "get rid" of these feelings, rather than have to experience them, as she now did directly. This was quite painful. Nevertheless, she reported that she was pleased and excited about discovering how much was going on in her and about the creative effort she perceived in this image production. She felt she had discovered an unknown potential in herself.

As this example illustrates, focusing on the interaction may at times require clarifying that attending to the interaction can itself become a form of resistance.

Attending to the subtlest aspects of the immediate analytic interaction becomes a way of generating a unique kind of intimacy and provides an experience in which the participants' awareness expands via the relationship as they clarify what they evoke and what they respond to in each other. This tends to generate new experiences of mutuality, of constructive intimacy, and of self-awareness. It also helps to focus the fact that analytic work generally requires the collaborative responsiveness of both participants, and highlights their interdependence and the fact that there are certain kinds of awareness (and certain kinds of experience) that neither can get to on his or her own. In effect, this way of working becomes not only a medium for analytic work, but also a measure of analytic achievement.

The kind of experience that becomes possible at the "intimate edge" does not evolve simply through time spent together; rather, its achievement requires an *active* effort on the part of both participants. It is not simply intellectual, in which case either participant would be involved in an exercise of his or her own cleverness rather than in a more personally profound exchange. Nor is it simply affective, since it is quite possible for either participant to be emotional without ever being touched by the other. Nor is it simply personal, since sharing intimate details about oneself might be no different from a recorded speech in which the words act as barriers rather than bridges. The essential qualities of the kind of engagement I am describing are *reciprocity* and *expanded awareness through authentic relation*. This involves a mutual willingness to risk the unknown.

CHAPTER 4

On the Question of Analyzability

As WE COME TO MORE FULLY appreciate the interactive nature of the analytic field, we recognize the degree to which the analyst's participation can influence transference-countertransference developments and the analytic movement that becomes possible. My focus in this chapter will be on how the nature of the analyst's participation can become the key to the question of analyzability.

The work of Fromm-Reichmann (1939, 1950, 1952), Winnicott (1949, 1969), Little (1951, 1957), and Searles (1965), among others, has been ground-breaking in demonstrating that certain kinds of analyst participation make it possible to work effectively with individuals who formerly might have been considered "unanalyzable." This body of work suggests that patients are too often blamed for what may actually be our limits as analysts or the limits of our theories of technique. It also suggests that in some instances the question of analyzability may hinge on our willingness to risk opening ourselves to the kinds of turmoil and stress working with more difficult patients may entail.

Unfortunately, if we assume for whatever reason that a patient is unanalyzable, this may preclude an opportunity for the patient to ever realize his or her own capabilities.

Winnicott's (1956) view in this regard is that "every failed analysis is a failure not of the patient but of the analyst" (p. 299). Stone (1954, 1961), Lipton (1977a, 1977b, 1983) and Klauber (1981), writing from a classical perspective, and Tauber (1954), from an interpersonal one, have argued that in many instances apparent "unanalyzability" may be an iatrogenic consequence of the analyst's "classical" technique.

What has become increasingly evident is that the establishment of a viable analytic process often depends as much on our capacities as on those of our patients. Certain kinds of analyst participation can be toxic and stimulate negative interactive developments, or at least fail to prevent them; other kinds can protect and facilitate an analytic process. This is particularly true in the context of more serious forms of pathology, where the potential for paranoid response is great. In such contexts an analyst who is experienced as too detached or ambiguous can evoke the escalation of the patient's anxieties, and the analyst who identifies too closely with the patient's experience can be terrifying in a different way.

In the context of difficulties in establishing an analytic process, it is important for us to question our technique and address its inadequacies rather than to assume the patient unanalyzable. In many such instances, modifications of technique do not constitute a violation of analytic integrity nor an abandonment of an analytic process; rather, they may be *essential* to establish or preserve an analytic possibility.

How can we structure the conditions of safety and help generate experiences that will be sufficiently positive to enable patients who have been severely traumatized and who are terrified of risking another catastrophe to take a risk on analysis, as well as on life itself?

Lacan's (1958) comment, "with supply we create demand," seems pertinent in this context. The question is, What kind of "supply" is required? What is it that the analyst must provide?

My experience has been that attending to the subtlest details of the analytic interaction (often of an affective nature) can be extremely useful where the potential for toxicity is high (Ehrenberg, 1974, 1982a, 1984a, 1985, 1990). Particularly with patients who are terrified of intrusion, violation, being coopted or coerced, dominated, controlled, or persecuted, I have found that clarifying in the immediate moment how the interaction becomes problematic and then making this the focus of scrutiny becomes a way to establish a context of adequate safety for both patient and analyst to engage the work in a positive way. This often allows for working "in close," at a level of relatively intense affective engagement, even with patients who otherwise present themselves as extremely detached and closed. Where the potential for interactive stalemate is great, *toxic developments are thus transcended or prevented, not by proceeding superficially or gingerly, but rather by actually attending to the subtlest sensitivities and vulnerabilities.* This process of meticulous scrutiny adds a new and transformative dimension to the immediate experience, creating a possibility of a vital and alive engagement, even with the most terrified and despairing patients.

Where boundary problems are prominent, acting out is standard, detachment is excessive, and primitive forms of behavior and communication prevail, treating the transaction as primary analytic data allows for each participant's sensitivities to the subtlest nuances of the other's participation to be clarified and tracked, and for differences in each one's experience of the same interaction to be clarified. This process of working at what becomes the "intimate edge" of the relationship can help to keep the relationship grounded, so that it does not become ambiguous and terrifyingly open to all kinds of unfounded assumptions, and so that patient and analyst do not lose touch with each other.

In some instances it can help the patient to grasp, in the immediate situation, the ways in which he or she may be structuring his or her own self-mystification or engaging in varying forms of masochistic compliance and submission or varying forms of projection or introjection. Particularly in the context of more serious forms of pathology, where primitive transference projections have the potential to evoke primitive countertransference responses, this kind of attention to interactive subtleties can prevent transference-countertransference from escalating out of hand and protect against varying kinds of unwitting collusive enactment. It also allows for clarifying the specific nature of vulnerability to enactment where this is an issue. As the analyst thus establishes that it is possible to work constructively with aspects of experience that otherwise might be felt to be threatening, repudiated and disavowed aspects of experience can begin to be reclaimed.

This approach is in direct contrast to any idea that one should allow a transference (or transference-countertransference) neurosis or psychosis to evolve. In fact, it becomes a way to protect against this kind of iatrogenic possibility and to maintain the safety and the analytic integrity of the relationship. By protecting the patient from the potential humiliation of "going out on a transferential limb," and acting out (or acting in) where this might be a risk, the analyst establishes that it is possible to work constructively with aspects of experience that otherwise might be felt to be too threatening. This allows for sadomasochistic fantasies, paranoid fears, or painful and potential disturbing memories and feelings to be rendered accessible and engaged analytically, where they might remain inaccessible otherwise, and for repudiated and disavowed aspects of experience to be reclaimed.

The effort is directed towards exploring impulses before they can become problematic. *In this way one facilitates a progressive, as opposed to regressive, process in which the patient is helped to engage in the analytic exploration of potentially disturbing or disorganizing aspects of his or her experience and to recover and experience painful affects and memories, without being subject to the kind of decompensation or acting out that can be humiliating and debilitating and without causing undue risk or provocation to patient or analyst.*

For many patients the opportunity to discover that it is possible to contain and deal constructively with aspects of experience that have been feared constitutes an important form of *new experience.* This has healing potential in itself and can become the basis for increased hopefulness and willingness to risk. It also contributes to the formation of a solid working alliance as patient and analyst become collaborators in the analytic endeavor.

My work with Sara illustrates some of these points.

SARA

Sara, a single woman in her thirties who felt traumatized by her experience in a prior treatment, ruminated for a year before finally deciding to call me. When she did she presented herself in a state of acute anxiety. She seemed terrified and was barely able to speak. She asked to meet on a once-a-week basis, and since it was clear that she was not sure whether she could even manage this, I agreed.

She spent the early months of treatment feeling nauseous, actually vomiting before every session, and worrying that she would vomit at the beginning of each session. She was often late and left early. When she was present, she usually sat huddled in her coat, literally shivering and freezing even on days when it was quite warm. I would offer a blanket when she did not have a coat, and I would offer to close the windows as she wished. She was profusely apologetic about her state and extremely solicitous of me. She worried about offending me or being too much of a burden. I emphasized that her anxiety was not something to apologize for or be ashamed of but what she was here to deal with. She expressed her surprise about my patience and concern, as well as about my tenderness at moments when she seemed to expect scorn and criticism.

She was truly puzzled as to what had happened in the prior treatment and barely able to talk about it. Despite efforts to reach an understanding of it, we were unable to do so. As I tried to focus on her experience in the moment, however, she produced many associations. I learned that she felt that her usual role in life had been to protect and take care of others, often at her own expense, and that this was what she had assumed she would do with me. She seemed to have no sense of entitlement to anything and no sense of any desires of her own. In fact, she seemed resigned to getting nothing and to wanting nothing for herself.

In the period following, there were some seemingly inexplicable moments with Sara when I could find myself becoming distracted despite her apparent great pain. One time when she began to cry and I found my attention wandering I felt horror at my own insensitivity. Though she seemed barely to notice, I told her that I did not understand what had happened. I felt the least I owed her was an apology. She brushed this off. I persisted and noted that as far as I was aware, this kind of insensitivity was not typical of me. I tried to engage her as to her ideas about what had occurred. To my surprise she replied matter of factly, saying that this was the typical way her mother responded to her whenever she had tried to talk to her about anything. She reiterated her feeling that it was no big deal to her now. I replied that as far as I was concerned it *was* a big deal, and that from my perspective her failure to understand that it was and her willingness to accept this kind of treatment from me—or from anyone—without a protest seemed to be part of the problem. She said nothing.

Sometime later there was an instance in which we were about to enact a similar scenario. I was able to observe her withdrawing precisely at a very painful moment and pushing me away so subtly that we would never even have realized this was so had I not been vigilant as a result of the earlier interaction. This allowed us to begin clarifying who in fact had done what to whom, and in what order—then with her mother, now with me.

Important associations to painful childhood experiences began to emerge in this context. I found myself moved to tears as she described the extreme disappointments and hurts she had endured and the ways she had learned to cut herself off in self-protection. In these sessions she described feeling, for the first time now, the pain she had not allowed herself to feel then. She reported that it was only now, through our interaction, that she could even begin to imagine that it could have been different then, and how much sadness this realization evoked.

The culmination of this early phase of our work was reflected in her awareness of an increasing sense of the distress involved in having to wait a whole week between sessions and a sense of hope and urgency about now getting to work as intensively as possible. She asked to increase our sessions to twice a week, and shortly thereafter to three times a week.

The issue of desire now became a central focus, as she began to want more from me and from the treatment and to let herself rely on the developing intimacy in a way she could not have allowed earlier. She revealed that up until now the idea of "wanting" and being disappointed had felt unmanageable, so that she had "protected" herself by "wanting nothing." She described experiences of endless betrayals in her family, and how *"understanding could be used as a weapon."*

Her experience had been that if she asked for something others would go out of their way to deprive her and to use her revelation of vulnerability against her. She elaborated that she feared positive experiences because they led her to hope. It was easier to expect the worst or to expect nothing. Then she would not be vulnerable to being disappointed.

In this context she revealed that she had a "secret" relationship with me in which she "took" in aspects of me and my room in a secret kind of way, so as to protect herself from the risk of rejection or betrayal that she might open herself to if she were to ask for what she wanted openly. She confessed that she had actually been taking tissues from my office in a deliberate way from the beginning of our work together. She had my tissues in the pockets of everything she owned and found comfort in knowing they were there. She also revealed that before my vacation she had taken a small piece of my doormat to keep with her while I was away.

Following this we were able to clarify a complex internal "code," which she thought she "got" from her mother: one should want nothing and take nothing from others. She elaborated the degree to which she had learned to "take" in such a way as not to admit she takes in order to survive.

She noted that when she was a child asking for things had often led to rejection and humiliation. This led her to wonder how she might learn to "soothe herself." She spoke of "taking in" my compassion in place of her "self-contempt" and expressed her concern as to whether this was a form of stealing.

As this was explicated she reported a complex combination of relief and apprehensiveness, as well as new curiosity and hope. She described feeling as though she *"had had an infected wound administered to and cleaned out."*

There were additional associations to the fact that she never knew whether her parents would be sober or drunk. She also described never knowing if there would be lunch money and how home was not only emotionally cold but also physically cold. There was often no heat because oil bills were not paid and no food because there was no money.

As she reported a new realization of her fear that treatment would work, and that if this were to happen it would constitute such a change that it would be frightening and she would feel indebted, there was a dramatic moment in which she finally felt warm enough to take off her coat.

About a year and seven months into the work, Sara asked to increase the frequency of her sessions to four times per week. The issue of allowing herself to "want" more, to ask for more, extended to her life outside of treatment as well, as she reported wanting a "better life," material things, especially clothes, and a social life. She also began to experience a very literal sense of physical hunger. She now realized that she had never let herself want before because she felt she could not have tolerated the vulnerability. She also began to be concerned about her weight, her health, and getting in "shape"; in addition, she initiated efforts to give up smoking, alcohol and drugs. In this context she reported the following dream:

"I was invited to a banquet, but I got involved in helping someone else who needed help, so that I arrived at the banquet late. When I first entered the room I was upset to realize that everyone else had finished eating and I was sad as I thought that there was no food left for me. Then I discovered, to my surprise, that there were many substantial things left and I was able to put together a really more than satisfying plate for myself."

In the period following she made many important life changes, including moving to a new apartment, which involved assuming a major new financial burden, and taking a new and challenging job. She was nervous and excited and quite conflicted, since these changes meant that at least temporarily she would have to cut our meetings down to once a week, but she felt determined to improve her life situation.

In this context she began to focus on how devastated she had felt by the many disappointments and betrayals she had experienced in relationship to her mother, whom she otherwise had perceived as quite caring. There were associations to how violated she had felt by a specific beating by her mother, which had been shockingly brutal, after which she had felt frightened and ashamed to go to school because of her bruises.

The result of this phase of the work was that she began to allow herself to experience feelings of anger as opposed to hopeless resignation, and she began to describe new feelings of deprivation and envy, as well as of wanting things she had never allowed herself to want before. She reported how angry she now felt that she could not afford to come four times a week, as she had in the past. She stated, *"I am afraid I will reach a point where I realize there is no hope for me . . . that you will know what I really wanted and was incapable of achieving. And I won't be able to continue to pretend that things don't matter to me that really do matter."*

Now she toyed with the idea of quitting treatment.

What emerged as we explored this was an acknowledgment that part of the motivation for holding back, and for the anger, was to keep distance so as to protect me. She worried that she would be putting me at risk to really let me into her inner world. It was a way to protect herself as well.

I expressed my view that it would be a shame to have gone through all of this only to give up now, and reiterated my commitment to continuing.

She told me how dumb I was, how naive, how grandiose, yet she seemed to be greatly moved and encouraged.

In the session following, she expressed fears that I might betray her. This concern about betrayal was, of course, still a live issue.

She reported a dream:

"I am in bed with a young man, much younger than me, whom I am 'crazy about' in reality. I am on top. We are not having intercourse but we are going to. At one point he says something about my being on top so I roll over so he is on top and he penetrates me. And then I remember we didn't use a condom and I leap up to get one. Then I am in an area where there are a lot of people and I never go back to bed again."

Her associations were that she was afraid of letting someone get her to the point where she would be responsive and she indicated that this was true in her relationship with me.

"I don't want to let somebody put me in that place and then be betrayed . . . maybe I feel too opened here, too vulnerable. Maybe it's easier to be frustrated and angry. That is like getting out of bed.

*I am afraid of being toyed with, being put in a place of being
responsive and then the other person doesn't really care. The game
is to get me to be responsive and then to hurt me."*

There were many associations to her alcoholic father and the
constant betrayal and disappointment she had felt in that relationship. She described his constant false promises to "get sober" and to
be a "real dad," as well as specific ways in which he had betrayed
and humiliated her and her whole family.

The following week she reported a date (in reality) with the same
young man she had been in bed with in the dream reported earlier.
They had had much fun together. She also reported a dream that
weekend in which she found herself *"laughing and laughing, so hard
and so happily. I haven't laughed in a very long time."*

In that session she stated that she had decided she wanted to
meet three times a week again despite the financial strain. She
elaborated: *"I am feeling more involved here and more anxious.
Then I get angry and feel very pushing away and disgruntled . . .
yet I feel grateful, though I never tell you that. What I experience
lately is feeling very lonely, wishing for a relationship. The grateful
part is that that is what I think I do feel, and what I should be upset
about, so even though it feels painful to me it feels right. . . . I feel
like I would rather feel that than have that whole part of myself be
dead or dissociated."*

In the fourth year of treatment, following a period of financial
stress in which Sara again had cut back to two sessions per week, we
had agreed to resume a three-times-a-week schedule. Unfortunately,
due to unexpected circumstances, I had to delay this by a couple of
weeks. I apologized, saying I was sorry, knowing how difficult it
would be for her, and offered makeup sessions, even though it was
inconvenient (which I did not say to her). Sara, who had been so
deferential and attentive to my needs in the early period of our
work, now was able to express her anger and resentment unequivo-
cally.

In the session following, however, Sara reported that she hadn't
wanted to come to her session that day and had even considered
quitting analysis altogether. She stated that it was too painful to
deal with disappointment because it reminded her of her family and
the constant despair she had always felt. Her view was that she

didn't want to "hope" because she was afraid she would only get crushed, here, now, as she been there, then. She stated, quite angrily, that she felt I was "jerking her around" as she had always been "jerked around" in her family.

"I was always waiting, waiting, waiting, for my father to be sober, for my mother to care. It never happened. I was always left bereft. My mother would say, 'This is not the right time,' but there was never a right time. Here it's too painful. I can't deal with the feelings. My life is still the same. Nothing has changed and nothing will change."

I pointed out that assuming there never had been a right time between us before, and that there never would be again, was not fair based on all we had been through together. I added that by acting as though I had been totally insensitive, she was insensitive to the fact that I had needs and problems of my own and that I had not canceled frivolously. In fact, I had gone out of my way to try to make up the sessions precisely because I knew how important it was to her.

She began to cry and acknowledged this was true. She stated that she was aware of how her reaction related so much to her relationship with her mother and provided more details about how this was so. She noted that the fact we could talk about our mutual feelings felt very different from what had gone on in her family: *"Whenever I exposed myself there I got crushed and humiliated and told I was a fool."*

She added that actually, even as bad as things could still be, she realized how much she had changed simply by virtue of the fact that she was no longer abusing drugs and alcohol, even when she was very upset. Then, in a playful moment, Sara acknowledged that, although she still got upset when I disappointed her, she knew our relationship was different and she affectionately teased that she *"had to take the bad with the good."*

Some sessions later, however, Sara's tone again was one of despair and blaming. She seemed to be preoccupied with her anger about the cancellations. She stated quite self-righteously that I had canceled and I had hurt her.

I began to realize at this point that I was feeling put upon and that I was offering to make up sessions at times that were inconvenient for me. As this began to crystallize, before I said a word about it, she expressed concern that she was getting me angry and that she was being "too much." I replied that as a matter of fact that seemed to be true. I added that I now realized that part of the problem for me was that, because I already felt guilty about canceling, I was especially vulnerable to her attacks and that this was my own issue. She seemed surprised at my openness about this.

We were able to establish in this session that we again were involved in a replay of the kind of entanglement she had gotten into with her mother. What became clear was that, instead of recognizing how unreasonable her mother's demands had been in the past, or getting angry when her mother became emotionally or physically punitive when Sara could not meet her demands, Sara got mad at herself for not being more capable. In some sense what seemed to be going on between us seemed to be a reversal of roles, in which I was blaming myself for not being able to meet all of Sara's demands, rather than questioning her expectation (or my own) that I should, much in the way Sara had felt with her mother.

My being able to recognize this had liberating effect on both of us and on our interaction.

I then noted that Sara seemed generally to expect that she should be superwoman and that she was always taking on more than any person could humanly manage and then blaming herself for not being able to do everything. She seemed intrigued as she emphasized how correct this sounded and how relieving it felt to hear this, and she began to document the myriad ways this was true, citing specific examples in the past and in the present, particularly at work.

We then were able to consider that the issue seemed to be how we each could be respectful of the other and of our wishes to be there for the other, *without violating our own real needs and with due respect for our own human limitations, without feeling guilty.* In this context she reported that she now recognized that her assumption had been that I had canceled thoughtlessly and uncaringly. This, rather than the actual cancellation, was what had been most upsetting. She then stated how much it meant to her that we had been able to go through the process we just had. This kind of intimacy was totally unlike anything she had ever been able to engage in with her mother – or with anyone else for that matter.

The following session she brought me flowers and stated that she had felt a sense of calmness after the last session that she had never felt before in her life.

Some weeks later, when Sara began to distance again and to express despair, *she* was able to acknowledge that this was "probably defensive," a way to protect herself from being disappointed. As we explored why she was feeling defensive and distancing from me now, she reported her belief that I preferred another patient, whom she had seen in my waiting room after a recent session. At this point, in keeping with her imagery when she had described her fear of being "jerked around" by me, I simply said she was being a "jerk," being quite clear about my affection for her.

I could have taken a more noncommittal stance; however, I believe that would have been playing with her emotions when she was clearly risking a new level of vulnerability and that would have been hurtful and counterproductive.

The following session she reported how frightened she was of the intensity of her feelings for me. Talking about our relationship, she stated, *"The more it goes on the more I defend myself. It's a defense like an air bag in a car. When I feel anxious or vulnerable, or in further, then the air bag opens up. I would probably be psychotic if I didn't have it."*

I replied, *"Maybe that is the key."*

Sara responded, *"That I would be psychotic?"*

I then replied, *"Or a fear of that."*

Sara's response to this was to reveal, *"When I am with another person, I often have the experience of intense fear that I am going to go crazy or act crazy and that I won't be able to take care of myself, and that the other person will not be able to keep it at a level that will allow me to feel safe and trusting."*

She continued, *"In my prior treatment I felt I was insane. I couldn't work through any of this. My fear was that I would have this dissociated feeling. . . . It's like beginning to go a little psychotic. I used to have it on dates, too. It was a disaster. . . . From early on, as a kid, I felt I was being driven mad by my parents. I would go for long angry walks alone trying to keep myself from going mad. I would have to get out."*

I asked whether wanting to quit here, as she often stated she wanted to do, was out of fear of going crazy if she stayed. And more specifically, was the fear that she might go crazy if she "stayed" in her own feelings?

She replied, *"I never stayed through those feelings before. I never stayed to see if I could come out the other side. It never occurred to me that I could. I always assumed I would just go crazy. It is a new idea to even think that it might be possible to get to the other side. To think maybe I can work this through. . . . "*

In the next session she reported that she had been totally exhausted after the last session. She felt exhausted in *"every bone of my body."*

Then she had dinner with her sister-in-law and *"something on a new level happened. At a moment when I would have dissociated, I didn't! I felt less crazy about going crazy in the moment!"*

As we went over the details of what had occurred she described her sister-in-law reporting how her son, Sara's nephew, lies, and how his father had yelled at him about this. Sara reported, *"That is when I would have gone off, I would have dissociated, because I would have thought to myself 'my brother is a liar.' Instead I told my sister-in-law 'but my brother lies a lot.'"*

Sara stated that the fact she was able to hold onto her own perception, and even to share it and to argue for it when her sister-in-law tried to make excuses for her brother, seemed momentous to her. She went on to elaborate how the kind of denial of reality that her nephew was being subject to was typical when she was growing up and *"could drive you crazy."*

She stated, *"I went home feeling manic. I knew I was identified with my nephew. I knew exactly what he was going through. . . . Then over the weekend I had a very vivid memory of something I had forgotten for all my life, of being the only person in my family who called my father an alcoholic. I might have been in junior high school. And he charged at me. He physically charged at me. And actually this happened many times. And when I would tell my mother he was an alcoholic she would not respond. She would not engage in it with me at all."*

I believe that the level of encounter and intimacy integral to my relationship with Sara, as well as the painstaking attention to all the interactive details to prevent the escalation of toxic transference-countertransference developments, enabled Sara to feel secure and safe enough to begin to engage aspects of her own experience that had been much too threatening and overwhelming for her to deal with earlier without dissociating. The fact that she was ultimately able to analytically engage very disturbing material without becoming "psychotic" and/or destructive, as she had feared, and to tolerate the vulnerability that went with the awakening of her own desire, allowed her to discover a potential in herself she had not anticipated, and thus became a healing experience itself.

It may be of interest that Sara, after reading this, reported: *"I think you really touched some deep emotion. I had an image, like an archeological dig, of a deep chamber inside opened, not with ease. It was like the antechamber of a tomb. There was all this stuff in there. Two people were standing at the edge of it. One was you and one was me. I did not want anything to be touched. I took the position that it's not right to open this thing up or disturb any of these things inside. They will crumble. And you took the position that they should be looked at and explored."*

In a session following, returning to this image, she noted her belief that if I had not been receptive to working with her, or if our work together had not been productive, *"instead of standing at the edge of the chamber and worrying what to do, I would have put something over it and weighted it down. I don't think I would have come up again."*

I agree with Sara that the analyst not only has the ability to facilitate the process but also to foreclose it — sometimes forever. It is a constant challenge to find ways to facilitate the former when the risk of provoking the latter is great.

CHAPTER 5

Structuring a Psychoanalytic Engagement

How do we structure an affectively vital psychoanalytic engagement with patients who present themselves as closed off, detached, inaccessible, and who are often considered "unanalyzable"? How do we achieve analytic "traction" in such contexts where traditional ways of working may not only be ineffective but actually preclude an analytic possibility?

By now it is quite clear that *psychoanalyst and patient can be involved in interaction without an analytic process occurring,* and that traditional criteria such as frequency of sessions, use of the couch, preserving the "frame" as traditionally defined, free association, even analysis of transference and resistance do not guarantee an analytic process — nor do variations in the maintenance of the frame necessarily preclude one (see Ehrenberg, 1984a; Gill, 1984, 1985, 1991).[7] The same intervention can be inspired in one context and detrimental in another. In some instances what has been traditionally defined as "analytic" may actually, and paradoxically, be counteranalytic.

From an interactive perspective, the critical issue inevitably is whether the patient is touched or reached in some significant way so that some *internal* process of affective significance is set in motion, and so that some internal psychic change (of an analytic nature) occurs. What facilitates a "psychoanalytic" process may have to be determined in each new context, as we learn from the work itself what kind of engagement and analyst participation is most facilitating *with each patient*. It may even be that *learning how to learn from our work with each patient,* so as to be able to be effective with him or her, is what is most critical.

From this perspective, determining what is analytic requires that we explore how analyst and patient actually do impact on each other, and that we recognize that our *understanding of this mutual impact can only evolve out of the work and requires the collaborative responsiveness of both.*

If we recognize that we always are limited by our own subjectivity and by our vulnerability to countertransference, it becomes clear that there is no other way to work than from *within this subjectivity.* This frees us from any illusions we may have about our potential for objectivity and enables us to appreciate both the interdependence of patient and analyst and the necessity for collaboration. It also helps us to recognize the importance of attending to the subtlest affective interactive nuances — nothing that occurs in the room is off limits. Thus the analytic field is radically expanded.

For example, exploring the patient's ongoing attempts to destroy an analytic possibility in the immediate interactive context, by delineating their impact on oneself and asking whether they might be in response to aspects of our participation of which we may have been unaware, is different from exploring these attempts as something the patient does from which the analyst is detached. If we use the awareness of how patients affect us to inform the work and convey an openness to explore how we affect them, and perhaps even threaten them, something very meaningful may happen. Neither patient nor analyst can retreat to some intellectualized exploration. Each has to deal with the reality of the immediate interactive experience as real — not as some disembodied clinical phenomenon. The very process of addressing aspects of the immediate experience transforms the moment and structures a kind of dialogue and intimacy that potentially can expand without limit. For some patients this might not have even been imaginable. Experiencing this kind of possibility can be affectively intense and tap into previously inaccessible aspects of experience.

Since we always have impact and are always being impacted, even if we are silent or unaware, what defines an analytic relationship is the analyst's openness to addressing and exploring the subtleties of these reciprocal processes that often are not acknowledged and addressed. Where patients assume that opening oneself can only lead to pain and disappointment, or even endanger oneself or other(s), this process can detoxify the field and provide a way to engage that is meaningful, manageable, and safe for both participants.

Focusing on the immediate transaction allows for either party's resistance to a collaborative relationship to become easily apparent and to be identified and explored, rather than enacted. This of course can become a collaborative endeavor itself, establishing that it is possible to engage collaboratively without violation of either participant. If we find ourselves uncomfortable with the idea of this kind of collaborative interdependence with a particular patient, this constitutes important analytic data.

In order to work on this level the analyst must be willing to put himself or herself on the line in terms of expanding the dialogue in ways that end up touching on his or her own participation. Often this conveys a commitment on his or her part to a relatively intimate engagement. It also conveys exactly how this can be achieved so as to preserve the analytic integrity and safety of the relationship. For some patients, this kind of engagement itself is a significant new experience.

Where analyzing fears, anxieties, detachment, and resistance seems to have no impact, the key to a viable process may be the analyst's willingness to take some kind of affective risk in order to reach the patient. This is consistent with a growing body of data from all psychoanalytic schools of thought suggesting that the analyst's more direct affective engagement not only can be constructive in advancing the analytic effort without compromising its integrity but may be essential. My view is that the combination of a rigorous analytic process and a vital, personal, affective engagement is crucial and that either without the other is insufficient. I believe it is the *integration* of both, and their operating not in alternation but in actual combination, as each becomes the condition for the other, that is essential and definitive. The integration of the affective and the analytic gives each more scope.[8] Either alone could not be carried as far analytically as each can be when it is combined with the other.

Winnicott (1969) stresses how important it can be for the patient to have the opportunity to discover that it is possible for the analyst to withstand and survive the patient's aggressions. The kind of engagement I am suggesting provides such an opportunity. It also allows for the discovery that neither participant need be damaged or diminished by expressions of positive feelings and experiences of closeness, which I have found can be equally profound. Sometimes just the discovery that certain kinds of intimacy are possible is significant. Similarly, the opportunity to discover that it is possible to make reparations and to have them be accepted when one has failed the other in some way (Fromm-Reichmann, 1950) can also be profoundly important.

At times the kind of engagement I am describing is so new in the patient's experience that it not only creates opportunities for discovering new interpersonal possibilities but also taps into internal capacities that may have never been utilized or developed. Stern (1983) makes a relevant observation in this regard. He notes that certain categories of experience "can never even occur unless elicited or maintained by the actions of another, and would never exist as a part of known self-experience without another" (p. 74).

Structuring the kind of analytic engagement I have been describing is, of course, as problematic where there is a florid transference as it is where the patient is detached and affectless. Intense affects can mask no less a closed system, and may at times make it harder to appreciate how inaccessible a patient may actually be. My experience has been that in the face of such inaccessibility, whether more obvious or less, one achieves a working alliance through establishing an analytic process, rather than the reverse. Only as the patient actually experiences how it works, and that it can work, does he or she feel ready to take the kind of risk that opening oneself more fully to analysis inevitably requires.

Some clinical examples will illustrate how the kind of participation I have been describing has been useful in situations where being able to achieve or sustain a viable psychoanalytic engagement was problematic.

RONALD

Ronald, a man in his twenties, was referred by a colleague after two years of treatment which seemed to have reached a stalemate. Despite acute somatic reactions to stress, including a severe colitis requiring several hospitalizations, and a prior history of obesity, Ronald was not aware of any emotional distress except in regard to his physical condition. He was zombie-like and detached. He claimed to have "no feelings," had little to say, and wasn't sure why he was coming. He would miss sessions and acted cynically, as though he were saying, "What's the difference anyway?" This was his attitude in general, toward work, and toward all relationships. When he showed up, sessions were characterized by a kind of vapidity and became as frustrating to me as they seemed to be for him.

I tried to convey to Ronald his impact on me, insisting that, although he did not seem to be concerned about whether our sessions were useful in any way, I was. Furthermore, I wondered why he bothered to come at all if he really didn't care and asked if he was aware of his effect on me. He seemed quite surprised by this and became curious.

As we explored what he hoped to achieve by coming, what he was structuring with his behavior, and how he experienced me, he in fact became more responsive and several things became clear.

First, he expressed his surprise at his impact on me. He had assumed that his stuporous detachment was a way of making himself "invisible." That it evoked such a reaction from me was a revelation as far as he was concerned, and he noted that it affected him greatly.

Second, he began to realize that this way of relating on his part was actually self protective and designed to preclude any chance of being hurt or disappointed himself. In this context he gradually began to get in touch with deep feelings of vulnerability, pain, sadness, and anger. This in turn evoked many associations to his childhood, which had been extremely traumatic. He reported memories of numerous scenes in which his alcoholic father had physically threatened his mother with a knife and of the terror he had felt as he observed these interactions. When I commented that even now he at times seemed to be glossing over the degree of pain he must have felt then, he reported that he was touched by my not accepting his efforts to minimize the extent of his pain. For the first time he could remember he was able to cry and to admit how hurt, hopeless, and desperate he felt.

The man who was untouchable and "did not care" was now very emotional. He was able to describe a decision never to be vulnerable again, made out of anger and despair as a child, and a feeling that he would rather be dead. The whole issue of his terror of feeling, caring, and wanting became accessible in this context.

ELIZABETH

When we met, Elizabeth, a woman in her twenties, was unable to talk to anyone or to manage the simple realities of living. She was barely audible in our first sessions, but managed to convey that she wanted to see me once a week and to find a group once a week, and she insisted that she would need medication. I said that it seemed to me this plan reflected her anxieties about throwing all her eggs in one basket. She readily agreed this was true. She had had several prior treatment experiences, had been through long periods of inability to function without heavy medication, and had previously been anorexic. Although she had had one positive therapeutic relationship, she felt most of her relationships in the past, in and out of treatment, had been destructive and sadomasochistic. She asked, *"Why should I assume this experience will be different from so many others?"*

I suggested that if she were going to give our work together a chance she would have to take a risk and not just go through the motions. I encouraged her to come twice a week and forego the group and medication long enough to decide for herself whether working with me could be of any value. She was terrified, skeptical, and cynical. We struggled with this over a period of sessions.

I suggested that it was critical to clarify her anxieties about treatment, as well as her fantasies about how she was planning to use it, before we could expect any meaningful work. The issue as I saw it was her cynicism and despair about the possibilities of ever changing or of ever getting help. We could easily go through the motions but she had done this enough times before to realize that it was not what she needed. In a sense, the first issue would have to be how we could work together in a meaningful and productive way, despite her own reluctance to allow this.

After several sessions she decided to forego the group and medication and we began to meet twice a week. She remained wary. During this time she studied every detail of my behavior, every facial expression, every change in posture, and confronted me with these as evidence of my lack of interest in her. I had to strain to hear her since she was virtually inaudible. I noted how sensitive and vulnerable she obviously felt, but also how challenging and demanding she was being in relation to me; it seemed that she was structuring our interaction as a test of me rather than trying to see if it could really be of use to her. This was specifically sabotaging the possibility that treatment would be of any benefit to her and was self-defeating in that it served to ensure another disappointment. In addition, the fears she experienced in relation to me and to treatment permeated every aspect of her life and experience.

In these early sessions she was able to elaborate how she had made it her goal to become impenetrable, to defend against dangers of being infiltrated, violated, or destructively influenced and altered. She saw this as a kind of heroic attempt to maintain her own integrity, similar to her anorexia. Her fear was that if she were to open herself even a little bit, be needful or dependent in any way, she would be totally vulnerable and defenseless. She documented many painful experiences of hurt and humiliation and talked of how she had been devastatingly disappointed and betrayed when she had taken risks. She had no sense of what her own participation was in these. Clarifying in specific detail how she contributed to the perpetuation of such experiences in our immediate interaction was critical.

Finding that something positive could come out of our work in this way was healing in itself and encouraged her to take further risks. Our relationship became increasingly important to her and she decided to come three times a week.

When I had to reschedule a session sometime later, she was devastated and felt betrayed. Her rage was such that it felt as though all we had achieved was now destroyed. She was unwilling to accept my apology and, despite my efforts to open this for discussion, she was absolutely unyielding, unwilling to consider anything I might say, and self-righteous about her position. I stated that I understood how painful this was to her, but I also emphasized how inconsiderate and punitive she was being toward me. I insisted that on the basis of our work so far, though she seemed to feel she had the "right" to now wipe the floor with me, I had at least earned the right for her to consider that my canceling the session might not have been frivolous or uncaring or irresponsible. Furthermore, if she felt she couldn't give me the benefit of the doubt, and even forgive me, then I felt I had as much right to be angry at her as she had to be angry at me. At this point I told her that I had actually canceled to go to the funeral of a friend. This seemed to break through the otherwise implacable wall of rage. There was even a hint of a smile as she commented, *"If you are poor and starving you can't afford to be generous."*

This permitted us to explore the extent of her voracious neediness and emotional hunger. There were many associations to and memories of how getting close in the past, particularly in relation to her father, had always resulted in devastating betrayals. That was her fear in relation to me.

She reported in the next session that she felt better than she had in weeks after the last session. She was "touched" that I was willing to "fight" with her. We were able to see that her usual way of dealing with things was that if she couldn't have all she would take nothing. She began to see how self-defeating this inevitably was. In contrast to the desperate, starving feeling she had reported earlier, she now began to describe with some embarrassment how "full" she felt in response to our sessions.

All the fears of being at the mercy of others when she felt close to anyone now intensified as she opened herself in treatment. She began to fear that I would make sexual or other claims and that she wouldn't be able to resist. She reported also that she had begun to have sexual feelings for me. She described how this had happened with every therapist she had ever seen, male or female, even those she didn't like and felt no attraction to. This marked the beginning of a period of work in which we were able to understand that the danger she feared from the other often reflected her own projected wishes. It also became possible to explore the degree of internal violence and "self-annihilation" she was capable of and felt the need to inflict on herself.

Sometime later, she began a session by acting out a pantomime that I could not understand. When I asked her to please explain she continued her behavior and ignored my question. This went on for an extended period, during which I felt increasingly uneasy and troubled about her state of mind. Finally she stated that she had been doing this to test me and to test our relationship. Her fear was that our relationship could only endure if she pleased me. Her wish was to see if it could endure if she didn't, and she felt her behavior was an act of courage and hope.

Once this was spelled out, I found myself feeling irritated at having been played with in this way and said so.

This seemed to affect her in several ways, some of which only became apparent later. At the time her first response was to state that realizing she could make me angry and create such a distance between us made her aware of how much she valued the closeness between us and how much that was something she had the ability to define. This was a revelation to her. She then described how she finally understood how she always tried to control the other person's responses by trying to please.

I replied that I liked her, which I did, and that her efforts to please me were irrelevant to my feelings for her. She started to cry and stated that she was finally beginning to understand that it was possible for people to be angry at each other without necessarily becoming sadistic toward each other or ending the relationship. Then she noted that she was beginning to see that she had a right to demand that she not be treated sadistically, but not that the other never be angry at her. Her anxieties about standing up for herself, her sense of desperate neediness, and the assumption that her survival required compromising or degrading herself in order to sustain relationships could now be further explored.

Having to confront and deal with the realities of my person and our situation also enabled her to recognize the extent of her intolerance of frustration and disappointment about an imperfect world and allowed her to begin to grapple with her difficulties in accepting not only my imperfections but her own as well.

Later, Elizabeth spontaneously told me that my willingness to live through these experiences with her and to treat her as a person rather than a "case" was what mattered most to her and made it possible for her to take the risks she did. My insistence that she participate in a constructive and honest way and treat me decently despite my limitations was crucial to this.

JUSTIN

Justin, who had been "free associating" in a seemingly diligent way, expressed frustration at my relative silence and his sense that "nothing" was happening. In his view it was up to me to get something going. He was concerned because I was his third therapist and he didn't want another "failed treatment."

I had a image, which I shared, of his prior therapist in a frenzy trying to reach him (he had described this therapist as very active and as letting nothing go by in an almost nagging way). I elaborated that my sense of what had occurred was that Justin had played along by giving his therapist a few "crumbs" now and then, but really no more. In fact, he had left with a sense of triumph that he had gotten away with something: he had outsmarted this therapist, getting him to "work" so hard to no avail.

I said that it was important for him to consider why he was coming for treatment now and what he was hoping to accomplish by doing so. I was clear that I was interested in and committed to working with him analytically if he wanted—but he had to decide what he wanted. Furthermore, I liked him as he was. If he wanted to change that was up to him. His response was that this really *"shakes me inside,"* and that he needed time to think about it. He added that he felt at a loss in response to my question. So far as he had been aware, he had only wanted to feel "happy," but he also realized that he didn't want to have to work toward this himself. That that was my job. I noted that no matter what I did it would be to no avail unless he worked with me. He responded with the following association:

"When I used to take acid in college, if I had frightening thoughts I would have an image of myself holding a bat. As the thoughts came toward me I would bat them away. The result was that none of them got to me."
This image helped to clarify for me my own experience whenever I had tried to engage him. Although I had not realized it until this moment, every time I said something to him I felt "batted away."

When I related this to him, he said he had to confess that *"I have been resting on my laurels."* He explained that by this he meant that *"I feel I have paid my dues."* His reference was to successfully terminating his addiction to heroin. He emphasized that he did not want to have to go through any further struggles in the present, and that he didn't want to be "bothered" by me or anyone else.

He then described the intense anxiety he was now feeling in response to the questions I had raised. It was much easier to concern himself with questions such as why he chose to sleep with someone on a particular occasion than to deal with questions such as what he wanted from treatment or from life. He had obviously allowed the ball into his court this time, and the affective intensity of his involvement was palpable.

In a subsequent session he was able to articulate that to admit any emotional involvement, to admit he could be affected, was humiliating to him. There were lengthy associations to an experience of having been molested as a child. He stated that this had always been his *"skeleton in the closet, festering away. I never dwell on it too long. I do the old home run trick and just bat it away."*

He elaborated on the shame, rage, humiliation, and self-blame for not protesting that he still felt about this incident. I noted the difference in the material since we had begun to discuss the need for his collaborative participation. He replied, *"What got raised for me was the key point about motivation. The idea that you presented to me was something I had never thought of. What do I want to become and to be? I have to talk about who I am if I want to get to who I want to be. I don't think I ever thought about who I want to be."*

Subsequently, he reported an unexpected meeting with his ex-wife, who had been an addict herself. He described experiencing a great deal of anxiety as to whether he could be seduced by her to return to drugs and realizing that he was not as "immune" as he had hoped. I indicated that this suggested to me that one of his concerns about getting analytically engaged was that it would inevitably put him in touch with the past and would reactivate the issue of his involvement with drugs. His response was that this was "on the mark." The thought of "opening up" emotionally meant he would then have to struggle with "stuff" he preferred to treat as dead. In contrast to the stance of going through the motions in the affectively detached way that characterized our earlier sessions, the concerns he expressed now were emotionally charged and full of meaning for him.

JULIA

Following a session in which she described strong positive feelings toward me, a relatively new patient, Julia, came in visibly distressed. She announced that she was freezing and depressed as she sat huddled and shivering in her coat at the far end of the couch. She expressed her concern about whether this relationship could "work," and stated that she needed space and that what she wanted now was for me to be quiet and leave her alone.

My first inclination was to respect her request for me to remain silent. Certainly there are times when any kind of comment by the analyst can interrupt a necessary experience or even foreclose it. But as time went on I began to question whether this was such a moment. In fact, I began to wonder whether complying with her request that I be silent reflected some form of collusion. Was she testing me in some way? Would my silence be understood as reflecting my belief in her fragility, perhaps confirming her worst fears? By remaining silent was I participating in a complex enactment I might not even be able to imagine? If I continued to remain silent, there would be no way to explore this. After much thought I decided to respond by sharing my dilemma. I noted that I wasn't sure whether to respect her request that I be silent, or whether being silent would be failing her analytically in some important way.

She said nothing. Encouraged by the lack of negative response, I then went on in a kind of monologue, noting that, even if she thought it was best that I remain silent, that didn't mean my silence would ultimately be most helpful to her. Or could it be, I wondered

out loud, that there was another question involved, which had to do
with her always insisting people do things her way? Was the issue a
need to control the situation, and me, and a fear of what might
happen if she did not? What if I did not remain silent and it turned
out this would be helpful in some way she could never have anticipated? Would that feel good or bad? If I did remain silent, would
she be relieved or disappointed? Or, I continued, was the issue
related to some feeling of not wanting to help herself or to be
helped? Perhaps she was invested in wanting this treatment not to
work? When she said she worried it wouldn't "work" between us,
was it the treatment she worried wouldn't work or was it her wish to
control me that she worried wouldn't work? Perhaps it was frightening for her to consider engaging in a process she felt she could not
totally control?

At that point I began to wonder about the fact she was "freezing"
and sitting there huddled up in her jacket. Was she waiting to see
whether I would respond and how? I continued my monologue,
wondering whether her experience was like that of someone who is
freezing, so cold she cannot not even get up to light a fire, or so cold
it might not occur to ask for help. Or was she waiting to see whether
I would offer some help? How would she feel were I to say, *"But I
am here with you. Suppose I light a fire if you can't?"*

She looked up at me with interest at this point. Encouraged by
her seeming intrigue, I continued. *"Let's suppose I just lit a fire."*

Her response to this was immediate and dramatic. In contrast to
the morose expression on her face up until this moment, she announced, with sudden animation, that she was no longer freezing
and was suddenly feeling very hot. She now took off her coat. At
that moment we both began to laugh. The ice was literally broken. I
then commented, *"I bet you didn't think you'd be capable of laughing like this today."*

She grinned.

At that point I commented, *"That was certainly a wonderful
moment."*

She replied, in what seemed to be an effort to turn down the heat
somewhat and to keep me in my place, *"It was okay, but not necessarily wonderful."*

I then asked how she felt about all the feelings that seemed to have been stirred by our interaction.

She replied that the very intensity of her feelings for me, both positive and negative, frightened her. She referred to the prior sessions as well as to the immediate interaction. She seemed angry as she stated that she didn't think I would be able to help her, even as she felt that I was her "only hope." She added that she was very frightened because she felt there was much at stake for her in this relationship, but not for me. She elaborated that she was aware of feeling very jealous of me. Her view was that I had it all, that I was successful professionally and had a family. At this point she lay down on the couch and very poignantly expressed her anxiety as to how could she know if this would work, how could she be sure she wouldn't go crazy. I was very moved as she articulated fears of being out of control, of losing her mind, and of my being unable to save her if this should happen.

Had I simply made an interpretation earlier that her reaction in this session, of wanting to be left alone, seemed to be a response to her discomfort with and anxiety about the feelings that had been stirred in the prior session, I do not believe it would it have had the same power as her coming to this now on her own. I also believe that my communication of my own struggle, my own investment in engaging with her, and my willingness to reach out to her even when she was pushing me away, were meaningful and significant above and beyond the actual content of what I conveyed.

JANE

Jane, a woman in her forties, reported what seemed like rich dream imagery. Nevertheless, my experience was that she was as detached and remote from this material as she was from me. I addressed what I experienced as her detachment rather than the content of her report and wondered out loud if what was going on between us now was similar to what she had often described in the past as the way she related during sexual experiences in which she "gave her body" but not "herself." This stimulated associations as to how disappointed she had felt during sexual experiences the weekend preceding. Her boyfriend had not realized how "absent" she was and made no effort to "find" her.

She became tearful as she then described how hurt she had felt by his lack of response to her "absence" and said that she took this to mean that he didn't "care." She contrasted this to my not letting her get away with this kind of detachment with me. She commented that she believed my response was a demonstration of my "caring." When we were grappling with each other, it made her feel "alive" and "real." With some discomfort she added that it also stimulated erotic feelings and fears towards me.

All the nuances of her complex game of "hide and seek," in which she actually made it difficult for the other to find her, as well as the feelings that were stimulated if the other person played along or not, could now be examined. In this context she was able to articulate her wish to have others prove how much they care by coming after her even when she fights and pushes them away. Her wish was for the other to want her enough to find her and hold her against her protests; this in fact "turned her on" and was how she had experienced my response.

She was then able to acknowledge the extent to which she was trying to seduce me to respond this way and the fact that she was only able to sustain a sense of being "alive" under these conditions. As this became poignantly crystallized, and the vicissitudes of the shifts between feeling "dead" or "alive" and her sense that these shifts were beyond her control were explored in our own interaction, she also revealed the erotic feelings she felt towards me and how terrified she thought she would become if she felt unable to keep me at arm's length.

I will not pursue the details of Jane's treatment here. My point at this time is simply that had I remained silent or responded to the content of her initial presentation, it probably would have been interpreted as evidence of my not caring, like her boyfriend, and would have led to different transference developments. And had I not pursued the effect of my response, all of this might not have been revealed. The dilemma, of course, was that any response would have been interpreted as a frustration or gratification of her fantasy. In this instance my effort to monitor what was going on between us was interpreted as evidence of my caring. Any other response would have been experienced as part of an enactment that had effects and consequences, whether I was aware of them or not and whether I was a willing participant or not. The challenge, of course, was how to create an analytic process given this set of realities. The presumption, of course, is that being alert to these interactive considerations is our greatest asset in such contexts.

Clearly the analyst's active participation, particularly when it is facilitating, can be seductive in its own way, precisely because it structures a new experience that may, for some, constitute a longed-for kind of gratification. It can, for example, be experienced as the fulfillment of a fantasy of being taken care of by a wise and/or powerful other. Where this is so, even an effort to analyze our impact can constitute gratification of this kind of fantasy. In some instances this can actually involve a convergence of both patient's and analyst's fantasies without either being so aware. Nevertheless, these concerns apply to any other kind of analyst participation as well. In some instances silence can also be interpreted as evidence of great caring, wisdom, understanding, or sexual interest, among other possibilities. This is precisely why rigorous attentiveness to interactive subtleties, particularly of an affective nature, is so essential.

CHAPTER 6

Dangers of Countertransference Resistance

COUNTERTRANSFERENCE WAS once considered a hindrance to analytic work. Now, though controversies still exist as to what constitutes its optimal use, and though there are real dangers of misuse, countertransference is recognized by virtually all analysts not only as integral to the analytic relationship, whether or not it is in awareness, but also as a potentially powerful and often crucial analytic tool. In some instances sensitivity to countertransference may be the only basis for tuning into the patient so as to be able to achieve an analytic possibility.

In this chapter I focus on the problem of *countertransference resistance* and elaborate why I believe this resistance itself not only precludes using countertransference data in facilitating ways in the analysis, but also increases the likelihood that countertransference will affect the work in less than optimal ways. It can constitute one of the gravest threats to analytic work.

Countertransference resistance often arises when awareness of countertransference requires us to face aspects of ourselves and our feelings that may be threatening. In this regard it is interesting to note that positive emotions can be as threatening as negative ones, as was evident as early as 1895 in Breuer's treatment of Anna O.

Countertransference resistance includes, of course, resistance to awareness of collusive involvements. It can involve identification and reaction formation, or defenses such as detachment, resistance to awareness of one's own affective reactions, or resistance to awareness of particular nuances of the transference-countertransference interaction. In some instances, however, countertransference resistance may involve resistance not simply to awareness of one's own reactions, but also to allowing any kind of emotional engagement with the patient. It may well be that in such instances it is more accurate to think of this kind of analyst "detachment" as a form of countertransference itself.

Alternatively, countertransference resistance may reflect the analyst's basic assumptions about the analytic task (see the position of Reich, 1951, 1960, for example). For this group the principle of neutrality is understood as requiring no, or minimal, emotional responsiveness on the part of the analyst; for others neutrality is defined in terms of how the analyst uses his or her reactions, the assumption being that these are inevitable. From the former perspective an analyst's emotional response can be viewed as evidence of a failure to maintain the proper analytic stance. In terms of the latter, the taboo on affective experience is seen as preventing the analyst from using himself or herself as a sensitive analytic instrument, and as precluding the kind of affective engagement that may be essential.

The latter view draws upon Heimann's (1950) observation that

> the emotions roused in [the analyst] are much nearer to the heart of the matter than his reasoning, or to put it in other words, his unconscious perception of the patient's unconscious is more acute and in advance of his conscious conception of the situation . . . the analyst's emotional response to his patient within the analytic situation represents one of the most important tools for his work. (p. 82)

My own experience is that the analyst's ability to respect and use his or her awareness of whatever is activated internally in the course of the work becomes a source of power and strength. From this perspective, even when we know our own issues are involved, we still can gain important information if we consider why with *this* patient and not with others, and also why *now* with this patient and not with this patient at other times.

An example comes to mind involving a supervisee whose work was surprisingly dull, even though he was perceptive and sensitive. With some trepidation he finally revealed that his energies were absorbed in a constant struggle to keep what he perceived to be his own "crazy" fantasies from intruding on work with his patients. When I suggested that it might be of value to consider how these fantasies might relate to what was going on in the room at the time, he was skeptical. Nevertheless, we searched for a possible connection; he was amazed to discover that his fantasies not only related to what was going on with his patients but also were quite incisive and penetrating and could be used to inform his work in important ways.

We have all had experiences such as one I had with one patient, in which I found myself having a fantasy of her arriving for a particular session with a gun, only to have her reveal in the very same session, without my having said anything, that she was having murderous fantasies about me which she had been terrified to share. In those instances where patients do not tell us such fantasies, sensitivity to this level of our own experience can be essential.

A common example of a kind of countertransference resistance involves those moments when the analyst may be overcome with sleepiness and he or she never relates it to being with the patient. Sometimes we become alert to this the session following when we find to our great surprise that we are suddenly wide awake. Only then does it become apparent that the sleepy response in the prior session was very specific to the earlier interaction. This of course allows us to use this awareness as a basis for structuring an analytic exploration.

We learn from these experiences that even when it may seem to us that our reactions are independent of the immediate context, that we are tired or distracted because of our own preoccupations, or that we are at the mercy of our own pathology, it is usually prudent to consider how our experience may be responsive to the interactive subtleties of the immediate moment.

Failure to consider that our feeling tired or distracted might be a response to some subtle development in the interaction may actually reflect a wish to avoid dealing with the anxiety of the moment or our possible anxiety about being vulnerable to our patient's impact. If this is the case then the real issue in such instances may actually be the countertransference resistance. In such instances tracking the interactive subtleties as they evolve between analyst and patient requires a collaborative engagement as it touches on aspects of the interaction which neither patient nor analyst could illuminate on his or her own.

Because patients tune into us just as we tune into them, how the analyst deals with his or her own countertransference obviously reveals a great deal about the analyst's relation to his or her own experience and about his or her trustworthiness and authenticity, which also has impact.

As early as 1915, Freud wrote:

> Since we demand strict truthfulness from our patients, we jeopardize our whole authority if we let ourselves be caught out by them in a departure from the truth. (1915a, p. 164)

In this regard, Ferenczi (1933) emphasized that patients

> show a remarkable, almost clairvoyant knowledge about the thoughts and emotions that go on in their analyst's mind. To deceive a patient in this respect seems hardly possible and if one tries to do so, it leads only to bad consequences. (p. 161)

Lacan's (1958) view is that "the inability to sustain a praxis in an authentic manner results as is usually the case with mankind, in the exercise of power."

Little (1951) approached the same issue from yet another angle. She wrote:

> To my mind it is [the] question of a paranoid or phobic attitude toward the analyst's own feelings which constitutes the greatest danger and difficulty in countertransference. The very real fear of being flooded with feeling of any kind, rage, anxiety, love, etc., in relation to one's patient and of

being passive to it and at its mercy leads to an unconscious avoidance or denial. Honest recognition of such feeling is essential to the analytic process, and the analysand is naturally sensitive to any insincerity in his analyst and will inevitably respond to it with hostility. He will identify with the analyst in it (by introjection) as a means of denying his own feelings and will exploit it generally in every way possible, to the detriment of his analysis. (p. 38)

The recognition that the patient tunes in to what the analyst feels, whether the analyst is open about this or not, and therefore is sensitive to any kind of inauthenticity, also has been emphasized by analysts as diverse as Rank, 1929; Fromm, 1941; Rioch, 1943; Winnicott, 1949; Fromm-Reichmann, 1950, 1952; Gitelson, 1952, 1962; Fairbairn, 1958; Tauber, 1954, 1979; Nacht, 1957, 1962; Wolstein, 1959; Loewald, 1960; Searles, 1965, 1979; Guntrip, 1969; Feiner, 1970; Singer, 1971, 1977; Levenson, 1972, 1983; Ehrenberg, 1974, 1982a, 1984a, 1985a, 1990. From such a perspective the position of Alexander (1956), as well as of some contemporary analysts, that there is benefit in assuming a deliberately predetermined attitude towards the patient would be considered to be untenable and to undermine the treatment process. It would preclude an opportunity to use the immediate experience as analytic data, and as a means to clarify very subtle interactive patterns that would otherwise elude awareness.

Nevertheless, the issue is not simply one of being "authentic." There are ways of being authentic that can burden our patients unnecessarily and that can derail rather than advance the analytic process.

If we accept the idea that denial or resistance to awareness of countertransference reactions can be detrimental to the process, and that awareness presents us with options we do not otherwise have, we are still faced with the question of how best to use this awareness. It is clear that use of countertransference data in any direct way with the patient is a delicate matter; unless handled judiciously, it can be counterproductive, even traumatizing. Any use of countertransference requires sensitivity, tact, and skill. This applies to active use as well as to decisions to remain silent, since there are times when silence can be as destructive, insensitive, or inappropriate as verbal interventions (Tauber, 1954, 1979).

It is critical, therefore, that we recognize that believing in the theoretical value – even necessity – of using countertransference is not the same as having the ability to do so constructively. In this vein, knowing one's own limits can prove to be the better part of wisdom. Nevertheless, the alternative of suppressing our feelings out of fear of mishandling a situation or of being seduced out of an analytic role may prevent analytic engagement. This kind of countertransference resistance may be a countertransference enactment reflecting our fears.

An example comes to mind in which a supervisee described feeling as though she were on "thin ice" with a patient. She was trying to find ways to "play it safe to avoid a blowup." Was the issue a misconception of her role? Or was it her astute recognition that she did not know any alternatives other than to remain silent? Perhaps she felt she would not have known how to handle a "blowup" if she helped to produce one. Or was she simply frightened of the patient or of her own possible retaliatory response? Did she not understand what the issues were? Was she tacitly colluding with the patient in a way that suited her own needs? Was this her way of retaliating? Or was she paralyzed by her fears of the reactions of her supervisor?

The truth was that the supervisee was in a delicate situation. The challenge was how to be able to use her awareness of her feeling that she was on "thin ice" in the service of finding a way out of her dilemma. The key turned out to be using her feeling of being in a bind as a basis for inquiry.

Often countertransference resistance reflects the analyst's sensitivity to the dangers of misuse of countertransference with a particular patient. What is required is learning how to refine our ability to use this resistance itself as valuable data.

An example of how our theoretical assumptions influence our relation to our own countertransference experience involves identification. The analyst who believes identification contributes to an ability to be empathic may not see identification as a possible countertransference issue, since it might be viewed as in keeping with an alleged desirable analytic attitude. Nevertheless, just as identification on the part of the patient can be defensive, the same may be true of the analyst. Identification on the part of either may be an expression of unconscious fantasies of fusion, merger, or wishes for sexual union. It may reflect desires to control, dominate, appropriate for oneself, devour, cannibalize, destroy, rape, violate, or desires to protect oneself or others from these dangers (Widlocher, 1985). Identification can be a means to flatter, idealize, seduce, or impress. It can be a way to avoid the analysis or experiences or fantasies of love, tenderness, hate, anger or any other emotion that might be aroused. In some instances identification may actually serve to avoid a real engagement, or to avoid provoking the anger of the other, or to avoid awareness of other aspects of reactions of oneself or of others that might be difficult, even traumatic, to acknowledge. It can also serve to avoid exposing the full extent and depth of the patient's actual pathology. What becomes apparent is that we can fail our patients though our "empathic" identification, the very response often equated with the caring analyst (Levenson, 1972; Beres and Arlow, 1974).

A particular interaction comes to mind. A patient described trying to deal with a very difficult situation as she imagined I would have, and how helpful this was in enabling her to cope with it. Her view was that she could not have done it without me. My first reaction was pleasure at hearing about her feelings of triumph and gratitude. Later, however, as I began to reflect on what had occurred, I was jarred by the realization that the way the patient had behaved was not at all similar to how I actually would have responded in that situation, and by the fact that this had not registered when she told me about it. Furthermore, I began to question why she was giving me credit and not crediting herself for her success, and why I was colluding with this by not questioning it. At that point I began to wonder what was going on; further, to what extent did my failure to be aware that something was going on involve a form of countertransference resistance?

At this point it became clear to me that any attempt to question what had occurred would probably have been experienced by this patient as a threat to her experience of being "one" with me. As such it would be viewed by her as a destructive rupture of our relationship, rather than as an effort to advance it. Penetrating the countertransference resistance thus allowed me to recognize my own countertransference collusion and to begin a more thoughtful consideration of what kind of response might be most analytically facilitating in this context.

It is, of course, important to be alert to the possibility that any effort to attend to one set of transference-countertransference issues, however valid, can be an extremely subtle form of countertransference resistance with regard to other issues, and or a form of enactment of other aspects of countertransference. Similarly, any decision as to how countertransference is to be used can be motivated by genuine analytic concerns or by countertransference impulses, such as impulses to retaliate, gratify, withhold, impress, protect, or to avoid other issues.

There are aspects of our reactions that can be quite elusive, such as feelings of great satisfaction or of defensiveness, or intruding thoughts or fantasies, or experiences of distractibility or inattentiveness. In such instances it is not only the countertransference that is at issue, but also the countertransference resistance itself.

In those instances in which the patient evokes the very reactions that are being attributed to the analyst, countertransference resistance precludes the possibility of clarifying these interactive subtleties and their symbolic meaning. Does relating in this way on the part of the patient reveal wishes to control and/or dominate the other? Is there an erotic aspect to this kind of interaction? Is it a kind of symbolic rape and violation? What fears might the patient be defending against by relating in this way? To what extent might it be in the service of an effort on the patient's part to cure himself or herself, or even the analyst?

Since countertransference resistance precludes understanding, we must turn our attention to ways of becoming aware of it whatever its form. One way is to increase our sensitivity to shifts in our own sense of identity as we work (Grinberg, 1962, 1979; Searles, 1965, 1979). Another is to attend to the patient's experience and interpretations of the countertransference (Little, 1951, 1957; Langs, 1976;

Hoffman, 1983). If we consider that the development of the transference is always to some extent shaped by the participation of the
analyst, then it follows that the transference itself can also be a clue
to aspects of our own countertransference of which we ourselves
might be unaware.

Let me present some brief case material to illustrate some of
these complexities in the actual clinical situation.

LAURA

Laura began a session stating that she was feeling a great deal of
pain that day and was angry that I was not suffering when she was.
When I tried to inquire about both her pain and her wish for me to
suffer with her, she responded angrily, almost accusingly, denying
that she had said she wanted me to be suffering if she were suffering.

I tried to focus on what had just happened, questioning why she
denied what she had just said, and why she was so angry and
attacking. She grew angrier. The following exchange ensued:

> PATIENT: I don't remember what I said, but maybe I didn't
> say what you said I was saying.
> ANALYST: I thought I had simply repeated what I had heard.
> PATIENT: Who the hell are you to be so confident in your
> perceptions?
> ANALYST: What do you mean?
> PATIENT: I guess I am saying who the hell am I not to be more
> confident in my perceptions.

She then said that she didn't remember what she had said. This
was followed by associations to a man she knew who was often
obnoxious.

> PATIENT: He expects compassion all the while he is terrible. I
> was wanting compassion from you like a hurt child.

I noted that in her association she seemed to be comparing herself to the man who was obnoxious when he wanted compassion.

PATIENT: If that is the effect I was having I wasn't aware. You are making big demands on me and I hate you for it. When I said, "Who the hell are you to be so confident in your perceptions?" you felt that was aggressive and my understanding was that it was defensive. If I experience what I do as defensive and you act like I have attacked you, that confuses me and distorts my reality.

I noted that in accusing me of distorting her reality, in effect she was challenging mine. I added that I was not saying it was not defensive. Apparently she felt it was defensive and I felt attacked. My point was simply that we were each entitled to our own experience.

PATIENT (as though there had been no argument): I have been agreeing with you all along.

Now I expressed my bewilderment, stating that this remark denied the whole process that had just gone on between us.

She then said that she was confused and asked me to go over what had just happened.

I went over the sequence of our interaction as I perceived it. I pointed out that all I was trying to say was that she had switched her position in the course of our exchange and then denied that she had done so: first with regard to her statement that she wanted me to suffer with her, second with regard to her initial argument that her behavior could not be aggressive if it were defensive.

She said she still didn't quite understand what had happened but it felt very important. She added: *"If I am being so slick I am lying to myself about what happened. It boggles my mind because then I don't know whether I can trust my perception of anything that happened before if I am doing this. I am very bewildered. I don't know if I am lying to myself or if I am letting you get away with something."*

She noted also that she felt good that she could talk about this without storming out in anger as she often had in earlier periods of our work. She added that there was something calming about having something concrete to address. She stated: *"If it's a discovery it's a major discovery and that is good."*

The following session she reported: *"I think the issue of switching things in midstream has to do with everything in my life that I switch attitudes on. One minute I think something is important and the next minute not at all. It's not a matter of malicious intent, but a whole life-style, the whole way I relate to my own experience. I can't know anything because from one minute to the next my perception is different."*

There were many associations to almost every aspect of her life past and present and an emotional realization that this was how her mother had related to her—changing truth, rewriting history. Nevertheless, she also emphasized that she felt I was not appreciating how painful it was for her to go through all of this, and she expressed some anger about how painful the last session had been for her, more or less putting us right back where we had started the prior session. This time, however, she was angry at me for being the instrument of her pain, while before she was angry that I was not suffering with her.

Then she related an incident that had occurred over the weekend. A man who seemed to be drunk was weaving along the sidewalk. Suddenly he made a quarter turn and walked right in front of her. She put her hands up, defensively. They collided and he fell face down on the sidewalk. She described how guilty and terrible she felt because she had had no idea how unsteady he was and because she was aware that she was angry at the intrusion. It was hard for her to tell whether he had bumped into her or she had pushed him.

She commented: *"It really throws me because we have been talking about all my hostility, yet in some sense I refuse to believe it. Yet it was terrible. Part of me feels horrible and brutal. What scares me is I can't even trust my own perception."*

There were associations to another incident in which she had hit someone. *"My impulses for real revenge and the fact I could act on them scare me. What if I really went wild? Anyone who had not seen what had happened would have thought I threw this guy across the sidewalk."*

Eventually she stated that a number of things were critical for her in these sessions. First there was the chance to recognize that her effect on me was different from what she was experiencing. She had only been aware of her own pain and defensiveness. The opportunity to realize her aggressiveness and its impact was new to her. Second, the idea that we could have a different experience of the same interaction was also new to her. Before she had believed that there was only one "truth." Third, the opportunity to see so tangibly how she could switch perceptions in midstream was shocking to her. There were associations to how her mother did that and to the fact that her mother also "lies" to herself a great deal. Fourth, she realized that part of her hostility toward me emerged because through our interaction she was being confronted with things about herself that she would have rather not seen. They were painful for her to acknowledge.

I believe that my insistence that we pay very close attention to what exactly was going on between us, as best we could determine at any given moment, was important in facilitating these insights. My painstaking efforts to track what was going on between us, in the minutest detail, to clarify how we got into the tangles we did, kept the relationship grounded and enabled the two of us to stay in contact. This process helped to clarify exactly who said or did what to provoke whom at times when things began to get quite confusing; as a result she was no longer able to ignore or deny her own contribution to the confusion between us and the ways in which she tended to forfeit her own reality by her own choice.

Clarifying the degree to which she would compromise herself in her efforts to "please" the other, and then feel victimized, helped her to feel less paranoid as she began to discover that she had more power than she realized. The result was that she was able to spell out her anxieties about our relationship, about how to know whether to trust her own judgment, and about her own vulnerability to influence. She noted with dread that she feared she would "lose herself" and not know whether she was feeling a certain way because of her own authentic wishes or because of her desire to please or to placate me. Even as she bemoaned how depressing it was to realize she still obviously had so much left to work on, however, she noted that realizing this allowed her to feel whole and separate in a way she had never before felt. She experienced this as a big step forward.

There were expressions of terror of needing or depending on anyone and of fears that she would not be able to survive disappointment and hurt if she truly opened herself to anyone. Details of

early experiences of having been victimized by others as a child now
became accessible.

(Going over these data years later, from the perspective of countertransference resistance, what strikes me is that the associations to
the obnoxious man and to the drunk might have been transference
allusions. My lack of awareness of this at the time may have been
indicative of countertransference resistance on my part. Were there
aspects to both images that had been threatening for me to consider? If her fear was of her ability to destroy or hurt, as in the instance
with the drunken man, it is possible that her anecdote evoked fears
of my own vulnerability in relation to her. Was confronting her with
her aggressiveness an assertion of my strength, meant to reassure
both of us about my ability to take care of myself [in contrast to
the drunken man]? Awareness of these possibilities at the time of
our interaction may have suggested options for me which the lack
of my awareness obscured.)

Months later Laura spent a session telling me how much better
she was feeling and that she was feeling "close" to me. She seemed
to be risking a degree of vulnerability she had never dared to allow
herself to experience before. Then she expressed concern as to how
she would know when it would be time to terminate.

In the following session she began with a challenge to me for all
the times I had hurt her. She continued angrily that all that we had
done was really useless anyway. She wondered whether she would
have done better with another analyst.

I found myself feeling angry and defensive. My reaction suggested to me that indeed someone else might have been less vulnerable
to her and perhaps more helpful.

She had obviously gotten to me. After some moments of silent
reflection as to how to respond, I finally said it was up to her
whether she chose to negate all we had done together or to make use
of it.

She responded by pointing to my defensiveness and reporting
that she was aware that what she had just done with me reflected
her pattern of managing to "get" people by really figuring out their
vulnerabilities and playing on them, even without necessarily being
consciously aware of doing so at the time. She then gave me a list of

examples and described how she felt her mother had done this to her.

Then, as we tried to determine what had prompted her to want to "get" me, what emerged was that she felt I hurt her every session simply by telling her that we had to stop at the end of the session. She continuously felt perplexed as to how to deal with the pain of loss. The idea of termination, which she had raised in the prior session as a result of feeling better, had apparently triggered this particular reaction now. Getting angry at me and negating the meaning of our relationship was one way she tended to try to deal with such feelings.

As this session ended she playfully quipped, *"I'll tame you yet."* Then she smiled warmly.

One could ask whether my assertions of strength in the first example and of vulnerability in the second were responses to some subtle cues from the patient as to what she needed and reflected some form of enactment that I still may not fully grasp.

What was being avoided in each of these interactions? The issues of her pain and her wish for me to suffer with her were separate from the issue of the denial that this was her wish and that she had expressed it. Did focusing on the denial become my way of avoiding her pain and suffering? If so, it would seem that my openness to one set of transference-countertransference issues could have been a resistance with regard to other issues that might have been more threatening for both of us. Similarly, in the second interaction, even as we focused on her potential pain in separation and on eventual termination, we managed not to deal with the feelings of closeness that were now activated. The anxieties that these aroused in her within the immediate situation, not only in the anticipated future, as later became clear, were profound and manifold. Was there countertransference collusion involved, since, beginning with the patient's initial remark that she wanted me to suffer when she suffered, the image of closeness being proposed was clearly an ambivalent one?

One could ask, would awareness of all this have made it possible to accelerate the work? Or, to what extent was the possible collusion necessary? Or, was the mutual effort to address all the complexities of what was going on between us the important process? What would have happened if I had proceeded differently or if she had indeed worked with someone else? To what extent was my willingness to get involved as I did, and to struggle with her as I did, critical?

I believe that sensitivity to the dangers of countertransference resistance can help us use countertransference to greater analytic advantage, as I will elaborate in the next chapter.

CHAPTER 7

Constructive Use of Countertransference

DESPITE INCREASING AGREEMENT about the importance of countertransference as a vital source of analytic data, there is much
controversy as to whether countertransference should be used in
direct ways with the patient, and if so what constitutes optimal use.
There is no question that there are real dangers of misuse.
Heimann's (1950) warning against the analyst's undisciplined dis-
charge of feelings to avoid the evident dangers of acting out, wild
analysis, manipulation, and the intrusive imposition of the analyst's
residual pathology is as valid now as it was then. She emphasized
that the analyst must be able to "*sustain* the feelings which are
stirred in him, as opposed to discharging them (as does the patient),
in order to *subordinate* them to the analytic task" (italics in original). Now, we also know that remaining silent about our experience
can be as much a countertransference enactment as any other kind
of analytic response. There is no way to avoid countertransference,
and attempting to deny its power can be dangerous. The question at
this point is not whether to use countertransference but *how*.

In considering how best to use countertransference I believe it is
useful to distinguish between the *reactive* dimension of counter-

transference, which has to do with what we find ourselves feeling in response to the patient that is often a surprise rather than a choice, and the kind of *active* response that takes into account this reactive response as data to be used towards informing a considered and deliberate clinical intervention. Silence, or any other reaction, can fall into either category.

For example: A supervisee presents material from the treatment of a patient who allows herself to be abused. The therapist is very actively critical of the patient for letting herself be abused by her boyfriend. In being so critical the therapist, without realizing it, actually responds to the patient no differently from the boyfriend. Therapist and patient are thus enacting the very same scenario as boyfriend and patient. In a sense one could say the therapist, despite her activity, is passively responding to some profound interactive pull. In this instance for her to have remained silent might have been a more "active" response.

The point is that active use of countertransference requires a thoughtful decision process with regard to how to use awareness of one's "reactive" countertransference responses to inform what will then become a considered response.

In some instances the analyst might actively decide to express the countertransference impulse in some direct way. In other instances an active decision may be made to remain silent. At times acknowledgment and discussion of a countertransference impulse, or of one's own difficulties managing or understanding one's reaction, or of the thought process involved in one's deliberations about how to use countertransference data, are potentially constructive options.

The point here is that the amount of overt activity that takes place is not indicative of whether the analyst is actively or passively responding to his or her impulse. In fact, the same overt response can reflect either kind of internal process.

I do not mean to imply that every response must be a considered one. There are times when our inability to stay on top of our reactions — even our losing it with a patient — may be useful. As Winnicott (1949, 1969) notes, the unflappable analyst may be useless when it is essential for the patient to know that he or she can make an impact. He cautions that there are times when an implacable analyst may actually provoke destructive forms of acting out, including suicide.

Nor do I mean to imply that the analyst must "understand" his or her countertransference reactions to use them constructively. In some instances willingness to let the patient know what the analyst is experiencing, even if the analyst may not at the time understand his or her own reaction, can facilitate the analytic work, simply because of the kind of collaborative possibility it structures. Even when the analyst feels at a loss, and when caution is appropriate, acknowledging that one feels at a loss can be an active use of countertransference. It emphasizes the necessity for a collaborative relationship and establishes a level of honesty and openness that can be significant in and of itself. It also leaves the door open for a creative gesture from the patient and allows the patient to help clarify what the issues may be when the analyst may not have a clue. In some instances this is the only way to access certain dimensions of experience and to realize the unique possibilities of the analytic moment.

This kind of process provides an opportunity to realize that it is possible to express and experience feelings one may not understand and to get "close" without fear of losing control. As it adds a new dimension to the analytic interaction it can lead to new levels of intimacy and to unexpected kinds of interactive developments. In addition, it establishes that understanding the significance of the experience of each may at times require the collaboration of the other.

The question at hand is how to determine at any given moment what use of countertransference will best advance the work. At times the question also may be how to remain analytically effective and alive when we are in the grip of the kind of countertransference that seems to threaten our ability to do so, such as when the patient may have deadening impact on us, or when we may find ourselves involved in enactments without understanding how or why.

The analyst's ability to use countertransference constructively, particularly in the face of more severe kinds of pathology, is often the factor that determines whether an analysis will have a chance of succeeding.

Some examples illustrating my own clinical explorations of ways
we might use countertransference constructively follow.

MICHAEL

Michael, a man in his twenties who had had some prior treatment, suffered from many somatic complaints. These, however,
were described by him as incidental. His presenting complaint was
that he had been and continued to be plagued by gory fantasies of
being physically injured, mutilated, or castrated by razor blades.

In the early phase of our work together the atmosphere of our
sessions was tense and oppressive; the content was dominated by
these gory fantasies, now in relation to me. He believed his fantasies
were unpredictable, had no relation to anything, and were proof
that he was "crazy."

He felt he had to hide what he viewed as his pathological fantasy
life from others, and he described a "morbid sense of isolation" as a
result. Being able to tell me all this, however, allowed him to feel a
little more connected and less isolated than he had felt with anyone
else.

In this early period of our work I struggled to discern some
pattern in our interaction. By tracking seemingly trivial minutiae I
was able to point out to him that if I seemed the least bit distracted
he was sure to experience a gory fantasy while simultaneously responding in a seemingly accepting way. For example, I had begun to
realize that if I yawned or looked at the clock he would inevitably
come up with one of these self-mutilating fantasies. At first he was
resistant to seeing the connection between his apparent loss of my
attention and his self-destructive thoughts. Nevertheless, the repeti-
tiveness of the pattern and my persistence in pointing it out each
time it occurred made it difficult for him to ignore.

Gradually, without either of us being aware, the sessions became
less oppressive. We were able to focus on the degree to which he
seemed to need to deny his real sensitivities, as he actually became
more conscious of them.

Sometime later I had to cancel a session. When he arrived for his
next session he made no mention of the cancellation but entered my
office with a strange look in his eye. He insisted that he had seen my

breast exposed as I opened the door to let him in. When I questioned him about this, he made it clear that he was not open to any exploration of his experience. He seemed completely estranged, even menacing.

After some thought I told him that I did not understand what was going on and that I felt very uncomfortable in the presence of what now felt to me to be a stranger I didn't know and couldn't reach. In fact, it was frightening. I added that it felt almost as though I had been abandoned by the person with whom I thought I had a relationship.

His response was dramatic. The wild look in his eye disappeared and he began to report with much emotion that he suddenly understood his reaction as a way of abandoning me to get back at me for having abandoned him. Now he realized how angry he was that I had canceled the prior session.

It is interesting to me now that at the time of this interaction I was obviously so affected by his behavior that I did not even make the connection to the cancellation (he was the one who made the interpretation). However, it is also interesting that my decision to be open about my reaction seemed to have been catalytic. I suspect that the process as it evolved may have actually been much more powerful in its impact than any interpretation I could have made had I been aware of the connection to the cancellation. There are several reasons. First, my openness seemed to allow him to experience a sense of his own potency at a time when his feelings of helplessness and impotence seemed to be more than he could tolerate. Second, it allowed him to make sense of his experience on his own and to recognize that there was an internal logic he had never comprehended before. Even though the content of his reaction — seeing my breast exposed when it was obviously not — seemed "crazy," he could begin to look at in a context and to become curious about his experience and its symbolic meaning, instead of being terrified by it. Third, being confronted with my vulnerability seemed to affect him in yet another way. Obviously, there are many more levels of impact that could be explored.

What is relevant here is that as a result of this interaction he was able to express how vulnerable he felt in relation to me and how terrifying and disorganizing it was for him to feel so dependent on me. There was a flood of memories of childhood fears, dreams and experiences, particularly of specific ways in which he felt his mother actually had toyed with his dependency on her and betrayed his trust. Getting into all of this material stirred intense emotions, which were not easy for him to deal with and which being "crazy" seemed to have been a way of avoiding.

In fact, this led to a period in which he began to express intense sexual and murderous feelings toward me, as well as anxiety about these feelings. Once he was able experience anger, hurt, and rage directly he began to make links to experiences as a child that he had not been able to deal with earlier. During this time there were many associations to his childhood, as he described similar sexual and murderous feelings toward his mother. As difficult as all this was, it was clear we were communicating and the scariness of that moment when he seemed to be so unreachable was gone.

Working back and forth from the immediate interaction to memories and associations elicited by all the emotions now aroused, we eventually developed a hypothesis that the feelings he experienced toward me (and anticipated from me) might have some basis in his actual experience with his mother. This led him to a courageous and dramatic confrontation with her. She confirmed that in the context of the great marital tension that had been pervasive in his childhood she had had suicidal fantasies, and that these had included plans to kill him and his siblings along with herself to get back at her husband. He reported that as she related this to him he was aware that she was being very sexually provocative. All of this was a revelation, and had great impact. His effectiveness in finding this out was as important as the content of what got clarified; the entire experience seemed liberating.

As he thus realized that his "crazy" fantasies were less "insane" than he had assumed, he began to be less terrified by them. In fact, he began to marvel at the imagination and creativity he now perceived as having gone into their construction. He became intrigued with unraveling the logic behind them and with the possibilities of the analytic process.

There was much associative material relating to father as well as mother and to siblings. In this context he became even more curious and more courageous, and this was manifested very concretely in his relationship with me. He became more direct and assertive; at the same time he was able to be increasingly tender, playful, and self-confident. Sessions began to change in the direction of a kind of playful exploration that became a pleasure for both of us. (I will elaborate on the details of the subsequent process in the next chapter.)

MARLA

Marla illustrates the kind of communication that can go on beyond words. In the first months of my work with her, I found myself in a perplexing state, which I had never before experienced. I could not remember her name when I was with her, despite all my efforts to do so. Nor could I come up with an explanation based on my own experience of what this might reflect about her, about our interaction, or about myself. I considered opening this up with her but felt in a bind because I did not feel it would be useful to say to her that I was having trouble remembering her name. My concern was that this would be needlessly upsetting to her and might become problematic. After continued deliberation I finally simply said, *"I have been wondering about your relation to your name."*

To my surprise her response was immediate and intense. She seemed shocked by my question as she exclaimed, *"How did you know?"*

What followed was a proclamation that she had always hated her name, that in her own mind she had a secret name different from her given one, and that this was the core of a secret fantasy life which she had never revealed to anyone and which no one, as far as she knew, had ever had any inkling of up until this moment.

Obviously I had not "known" in the sense of knowing what she thus revealed. All I knew was that there was something I was responding to that seemed to focus on her name, and this informed my intervention.

JOHN

In a session just prior to my taking off one week, a relatively new patient, John, talked about quitting. He said that he really did not see any value to continuing treatment unless there was "something going on in his life" that he could talk about. I asked whether he thought his response might be related to the fact that I would be away for a week. He insisted that it was not. He spoke, not really talking to me but at me, and without any affect. What struck me was my own reaction. I found myself feeling pleased by the thought of a free hour, and was aware of an impulse to say nothing further in the hope that he would decide to leave.

At first I was surprised and almost guilty about having such a reaction. When I began to consider that this might be important data about the situation, I found that I was able to make an internal shift myself. At that point I was no longer "put off," but actually concerned with how to use this. After some thought I decided to tell him my reaction, emphasizing that I did not see his reaction of wanting to quit, or mine of wanting to let him, as a basis to disengage but rather as important and necessary data for our work. I also wondered out loud whether my response was unique in his experience.

He seemed visibly shaken and began to cry. He remarked that this was exactly what he did seem to evoke in everyone. He then described a date he had had the same week and other incidents during which similar interactions occurred. He now described with much feeling the pain he felt about not being able to "connect" with anyone and not understanding why. I was moved by his openness and by the intensity of his feelings and told him so. He stated how touched he was by my response and expressed a new sense of hope that treatment might be helpful.

In the following session it began to be clear that he had found it difficult to allow any relationship to be important to him, especially ours. He expressed a desire to be totally self-sufficient. He didn't want to have to ever rely on anyone who could possibly disappoint, hurt, or abandon him (as I was now about to do for one week). This patient, whose mother had died when he was a very young child, described now how he wanted to be able to *"survive in a foxhole alone."*

As we pursued these issues there were further associations to his terror of being "dumped" by me or anyone, should he become involved. He noted that when he does get involved it becomes so intense and out of control that it is terrifying. When one girlfriend broke up with him he lost forty pounds and had a "breakdown." He stated that now, *"I have it so that even if a girlfriend were able to tell me to get lost I would be totally unphased."*

The issue of his cynicism and despair, his tendency to give up without trying—not only in treatment but also in life in general—could be addressed. When I emphasized my belief that it would be possible for him to work some of this out, he began to cry.

Although there were many expressions of ambivalence, at this point he was willing to entertain the idea that my vacation might have been more significant than he had allowed himself to consider before. Moreover, he was able to reveal a deep sadness, a sense of fearfulness, of neediness, and of anxiety about revealing all this to me.

We were now engaged in what felt to be a very intense way.

IAN

Ian, a young man in his twenties, spoke at length in rapturous tones about how much he cared about me and valued his treatment. In contrast to expressions of caring that move me, this display did not. In fact, it made me quite uneasy, although I was not immediately clear why.

The countertransference dilemma I found myself in was that I feared a challenge to his authenticity might be shattering. Yet to say nothing felt like complicity. (What seems obvious now would have been to comment about my uneasiness in response to what he was saying. But I was so uneasy at the time that it did not occur to me.) The sessions continued similarly and I struggled in my own mind with the question of whether and how to intervene.

Then one session, instead of telling me how much he cared about me, he began to express concern that I might find him boring, that I didn't care, that I didn't like him, that I must dread the hours when he comes. When I inquired about this he said it was because he finds himself boring and doesn't like himself very much. It finally dawned on me that what I was reacting to was that when he spoke about himself and his feelings he seemed to dramatize the slightest emotion. At that point I stated that it seemed as though he had doubts about his own capacities to feel. I also wondered if he felt he had to impress and convince both himself and me that he could feel something. He seemed receptive. I noted that if these impressions were accurate two issues were now focused: his efforts at pretense, and his anxiety about his capacity to feel.

Ian's response was a long silence, during which he seemed choked with emotion. Finally he said that what I had stated was true. I suggested that if this were the case it would be much more productive to try to deal honestly with this as a problem to work on in treatment, rather than pretend it were not true, since that would abort the opportunity to try to resolve it. There were many associations in response, describing his awareness that this was a characteristic way of relating for him, even though he had never been able to articulate it this clearly himself.

My intervention apparently had an impact on both of us. I was no longer uneasy and felt more related to him than I had felt during the whole period preceding.

In the following session he remarked that he was very frightened of me and what he might find out in analysis. But he said he felt the last session had been extremely important, and he was relieved that I had understood. In contrast to my earlier reaction of being left cold, I was moved. It felt like communication between us was now authentic and open.

In a very intense session sometime later he was able to acknowledge that he thought he was afraid to know what he felt or to develop feelings because he worried if he did he might develop intense sexual feelings for me and wouldn't know what to do with them. He worried that his feelings would get out of control and he would not be able to set any limits. He reported that after the last session he had had the thought that I would call him up and say, *"Why don't you run away with me?"* and that he would.

He noted that during the last session he had noticed that my haircut made me seem younger. For a moment he thought I was younger than he (I am sixteen years older). He said that when he had commented that he liked my haircut I had seemed pleased. That conveyed to him a sense of my vulnerability, which made him feel close to me. But he worried that I would be hurt if he said I was vulnerable. He expressed concern that I would find out how crazy he is and wouldn't want a connection with him. Still, it felt endearing to realize my vulnerability. He worried about saying this to me. He worried that he didn't see me as I am.

The associations continued. He stated that he was very frightened to feel he depended on, relied on, or needed me. Then he had to deal with his fears that I might leave, that I might quit my practice. He felt very vulnerable. It was just as scary to think I might value him. Then he believed he had to live up to some expectation or I would lose interest. He stated that he was surprisingly less paranoid with me than he was with most people. Also, he was starting to develop a more intense fantasy life about me. He fantasized about what I think about and what I am like in my personal life. He expressed one concern as follows:

"I am not sure if it happened already, or I am afraid it will happen. It's hard to tell you. My concern is that at the moment of orgasm I will think of you. That will completely freak me out. I don't know if it actually happened already or not. Once that happened where I thought of my mother at the point of orgasm. That really freaked me out."

In subsequent sessions he spoke about feeling dependent, scared, falling in love with me. He wondered if the analysis was an exercise in masochism. He expressed concern about issues of power and control. He reported explicit sexual fantasies about me with embarrassment, worrying I would be horrified. In the fantasies sometimes he was able to turn me on. Sometimes this was unimaginable to him. This led to associations to his mother.

"She is really attractive but I can't imagine her being turned on. I can't imagine she ever had sex in her life. There is something weird about the knowledge that in real life you and I will never have sex. It feels disappointing and comforting at the same time."

An associational process was now launched that continued over many weeks. I emphasize this because the aim of the kinds of interventions I have been describing is to facilitate this kind of process. Once it is in motion it is just as important not to get in the patient's way.

MARILYN

In a particular session with Marilyn, I found myself unable to stop yawning. She indicated that she was hurt by this and felt angry. I noted that since I was not always this way with her it was important to consider what this reflected about what was happening between us now. I asked if it felt familiar in some way and noted that, though I myself was not clear what was going on, it seemed very similar to experiences she had described in relation to her mother.

Her associations to this were she had had great difficulty keeping her mother's attention. She felt it was only possible to be with her mother on her mother's terms. There was no way to be with her mother and express her own needs or concerns and keep mother's interest. She elaborated that eventually she reached a point where she felt clear that to be herself would be "too boring" and she would lose her mother's attention. She began to "invent a self" to engage her mother with. Later in life she would fake orgasms or pretend to enjoy sex when she did not in a similar pattern.

At this point she began to cry, saying she was afraid her "real self" was "no good" and that she didn't want to find out.

I in turn was now very engaged and no longer yawning. I remarked on this to her. It was quite clear to her that she had reached me. She noted that the fact that my responsiveness now was clearly not out of compliance with her demand for my full attention or with my view of my role as an analyst, but because it was genuinely felt, had great meaning to her. In addition, the fact we could talk about this explicitly, virtually as it was occurring, seemed to be as meaningful as its occurrence.

In this encounter, it became apparent to both of us that my yawning had been in response to her effort to play a role, whereas when she was being genuine I really did respond.

This led to her realizing how frightened she generally felt to risk being genuine, since this held the possibility of rejection. Nevertheless, she now also was able to see that playing a role perpetuated her state of isolation and despair by precluding the possibility of a positive connection.

Unraveling all this turned out to be quite illuminating; neither of us could have anticipated the results. It opened many questions about the subtleties of her interaction with her mother that she still did not quite understand. How were we involved in a replay? To what degree had we gotten beyond into something new? Had I denied or tried to hide my reaction I believe we would not have explored these areas. (What I did not do at that time was explore whether her role playing was in response to some aspect of my own participation of which I was unaware. I would certainly try to pursue that kind of exploration now.)

Some months later, in a very moving session, Marilyn spoke about how inadequate she felt professionally. At this time she noted that she recognized that being able to admit this, rather than pretend otherwise, reflected what she perceived to be great progress. As she articulated her fears about feeling so exposed, she noted that at the same time she felt relief in being this open. It opened the way for her to begin to learn to become more competent. At this moment she understood how the pretense had in fact worked to perpetuate her inadequacy and isolation, and she became aware of options she had never realized before.

What was technically critical from my perspective was that I did not simply say, "I am yawning because you are boring me." That would not have facilitated the process in any way. Rather, I said, "Let's look at why this is happening now, since it is not my usual reaction to you." This opened up a way to move forward analytically, as it structured a collaborative process. We transcended the isolation inherent in acting and reacting by looking at, rather than simply responding to, the very pushes and pulls operative earlier. My willingness to be open about my lack of understanding with regard to my own reaction also seemed meaningful to her and possibly contributed to her opening up about her own feelings of inadequacy later.

JEFF

Jeff responded to an interruption of treatment of several weeks' duration, due to my illness, with striking indifference. At one point when I spoke to him on the phone to let him know I would be out longer than I had anticipated, he cavalierly commented, "Have a nice recuperation." My first reaction was to feel surprised and hurt, and then defensively cynical. I began to think how naive I had been to have assumed he might care. But as I thought more about this, I began to wonder whether I was actually off base now in assuming that he simply had no feelings at all. Had he been deceiving me before? Was he deceiving me now? Had I been deceiving myself to think he had any feelings for me before? Had I had been too quick to accept his indifference now?

When we resumed work, although he wanted to go on as usual, I felt it was important to address these questions. I stated that I had felt truly puzzled by his cavalierness on the phone and by the lack of any emotion, positive or negative, about my illness and about the break it had caused in our work. I added that I realized it was possible I was off base in being surprised by his response, but it seemed equally possible that he was defending against his own feelings in some way. My view was that there was something going on between us that one of us would have to come to terms with, though I was not at all clear which one of us that was. There were two issues as I saw it: one was the impact of my illness; the other was the nature of our relationship. If my illness really left him as unaffected as it seemed to have done, then it opened to question the nature of our relationship, at least as I had understood it.

In response to my expression of confusion and surprise about his seeming indifference, he took a defensive posture, saying that he had not wanted to be intrusive, that he had assumed I would be all right, that he had not been worried.

We seemed to be getting nowhere, and I became increasingly aware of not knowing whether to trust him or not.

His father had died when he was a very young child. I suggested that this might be relevant to understanding his response now. Was this his way of dealing with illness and the possibility of loss in general? He replied that this seemed a reasonable line of inquiry; nevertheless, there was no real affective response.

Then it occurred to me that perhaps my feeling that I could not trust him and my internal feelings of cynicism were the key to what was going on with him. At that point I said to him that perhaps the issue was that he didn't trust me or our relationship. To my surprise he responded to this with much emotion, stating, *"No one touches me. I don't trust anyone or any relationship. I am self-contained."* He seemed to surprise himself with the intensity of his own feelings as he said this.

He then began to speak of his confusion about the boundaries of our relationship. *"Is it just professional or is it personal?"*

He then noted that, although he had assumed that I didn't care about him at all except out of some sense of professional obligation, he was actually very touched to realize that I had been upset by his reaction and that I had given it so much thought. He added that he would not have imagined that I would have been concerned about him when I was ill, and how sorry he was that he had upset and apparently disappointed me. He then expressed a wish to make it up to me. I was moved by his emotion but troubled by the fact that he now seemed to feel guilty and apologetic, and said so. I emphasized that my concern had been simply to clarify what was going on between us, as much for my benefit as for his. My view was that if I had read him wrong I wanted to know about it, and if we were really so out of touch with each other, for whatever reason, that was a serious problem which we needed to address.

He was now more open than he had ever been, as he began to describe his fears about letting anyone penetrate his "wall." His associations focused on his relationship with his mother and on what it was like to grow up without a father. Details began to emerge that led us both to think that his mother had never recovered from the loss of her husband. He thus had lost the mother he had known before as well as his father when his father died. Arriving at this helped us to begin to appreciate how little he had come to ask for emotionally in his relationships and how little he assumed it was possible to expect. It also enabled us to clarify ways he may have colluded in perpetuating certain kinds of deprivation in his relationships without even understanding that he was doing so. There were further insights as to ways this continued to be true in his current relationships, including his relationship with me.

MAX

Max generally began his sessions talking about things that seemed promising. The problem was that what appeared so promising at first inevitably seemed to go nowhere. If I tried to address this or to respond in any way, he became angry at me for interrupting his flow. Gradually I began to feel like a captive audience, without quite even being aware of how frustrated I was becoming. Instead, my experience was that it became more and more difficult to remain attentive, that I would increasingly find myself drifting off into my own thoughts and fantasies, that I made no effort to resist this, and that I did not even want to. There was some sense that if this was what he wanted I would give it to him, in spades. As this became clearer to me, however, I began to be intrigued with what indeed was going on, and at that point I insisted that we try to understand the process. Though he was no less resistant than before, I was no longer willing to be put off. In this context we were able to clarify a scenario that was more or less implicit in his mind.

He seemed to feel, *"I want you to help me. I'm afraid you won't. I'm not going to risk being disappointed, and I'm not even going to allow an opportunity to be in a position to be disappointed."*

In effect he had more or less decided, without actually recognizing it at the time, that *"I can't dare be real with you or allow you to be real for me, or allow our interaction to be significant in any real way."*

Once this was clarified, the work came alive in a way it had not been before, and there were many associations to his relationship with his father, and the pain and anger that this had involved. In this context it was possible to see that some of what I had been experiencing in relation to him was similar to his experience with his father.

SARA

Sara expressed great anxiety as the time of my summer vacation was approaching in the second year of our work. In the preceding year she had cut a piece of my doormat to keep with her while I was away. It was only many months later that she had told me about this. At that time she had noted that in her experience asking for things had generally led to rejection and humiliation. She felt that when she asked for something some others would specifically go out of their way to deprive her and to use her revelation of vulnerability against her. She was extremely open and moving as she articulated how vulnerable she felt telling me this (see Chapter 4).

As we explored her feelings now about the impending interruption in our work, I found myself having an intense desire to give her something before I left for vacation. In a particular session in which she was describing how much she enjoyed a particular pocket knife she owned, the impulse suddenly concretized for me. I had a folding Chinese scissor which I was particularly fond of, and I realized this would probably be just the kind of thing she might love to have. I wondered about the obvious symbolism of offering a tool for cutting, in light of the fact that she had cut a piece of my doormat last year.

As all this went through my mind, the impulse to give her the scissors only became more intense. Its sheer compellingness made me wary, and yet I could not get past it. It was much harder not to give her the scissors at this point than it would have been to give in to my impulse to do so. My efforts to understand what this might reflect about what was going on between us and what needed to be addressed led me nowhere. At this point I felt clear that something important was involved, and I decided to proceed by telling her about my impulse and about my analytic dilemma, without actually giving her the scissors.

She was delighted with the fact I wanted to give her something, with the fact I was willing to share the fantasy with her, with the idea of the scissors. She said it would have been perfect.

The following session, however, she was troubled about whether this was a "tease," whether I was somehow playing with her. I began to wonder whether it would have been better not to have raised this with her at all. I shared my concern with her. As we struggled with all the feelings this evoked, there were many charged associations. Memories were stirred of promises that were not met in her childhood and of how betrayed she inevitably felt. New details of very painful interactions with her parents and with each of her siblings now emerged.

She described with much emotion how much she had wanted *"something, anything,"* from her mother and had always been devastatingly disappointed, and how despairing she had felt when her mother died and there was nothing left for her.

As we pursued what it would have meant if I had given her the scissors, and the fact that I had not but had told her of my wish to do so, I told her that it would have been much easier for me to give her the scissors than it had been not to, and that my decision not to act on my impulse was based on my wish to protect the analytic integrity of our relationship. I added that one consideration that seemed relevant was my own sense that, if I could act on my positive impulse, then wouldn't that mean I could also act on a negative impulse at some future time?

There is obviously no way to know what might have emerged had I not been explicit about the countertransference, or had I given her the scissors. At the time I felt sharing my internal struggle with her as I did was an enactment of my impulse to give her something but an effort to do so in an analytically safe way, even as I also worried whether I was involved in a kind of tantalizing enactment without understanding this was so.

This interaction, for better or worse, seemed not only to open a very productive and profoundly emotional exploration but also to contribute to a sense of greater intimacy between us and trust in our evolving relationship. The boundaries of what we could talk about with each other were expanded. I believe the new experience of interpersonal possibility that this provided was significant in and of itself.

MARJORIE

Marjorie, a child of three years and nine months, was brought to a low cost clinic for treatment in a mute and zombielike state. Her eyes had a glazed and vacant stare and she was totally unresponsive to anything or anyone around her. This pattern had developed after her mother was hospitalized for a serious illness, suggesting that this was a reaction to trauma and not a state that had been genetically or congenitally determined. Nevertheless, the presenting question was whether she was "retarded." We began to meet on a twice weekly basis.

At the outset I found myself trying everything I could think of to engage her, to no avail. In session after session, week after week, she seemed to look through me rather than at me, seemingly unaware of my presence. I was then a candidate in training, so I felt particularly vulnerable to this experience of total impotence.

Finally, at a point when I had begun to despair totally, and when it seemed to me that things could not get much worse, I decided to take a risk. Well aware that this might be considered outrageous, I quietly said to her something on the order of *"I feel at a total loss. I don't know how you feel but I feel so terrible I want to scream and I am going to."* And I proceeded to scream.[9]

Her response was dramatic. She began to shake from head to toe. For the first time, the glazed look left her eyes. She now looked terrified. But she also looked accessible in a way I had never seen before.

At that point I tried once more to convey my wish to help her with her sadness and pain, my understanding of how terrible someone could feel, and my own sadness at how hard it had been between us. This time, when I encouraged her to tell me or to show me her feelings and indicated that she might want to use the dolls toward this end, she was responsive.

What she in fact did with the dolls was to set them up to represent the members of her family. I told her that it was perfectly safe to express any feelings she wanted to in this kind of play and that this would not hurt anyone in reality. She was hesitant but seemed intrigued.

She then began to play out killing each of the dolls: with knives, guns, marbles, and whatever else she found in the room. She then wanted to run out to the waiting room. I asked if she wanted to see if her mother was still alive after she had "murdered" her in our session. She did run out and returned, seeming pleased by the fact that her mother was indeed perfectly fine.

She repeated the attacks on the dolls representing members of her family with increasing fervor over the next few sessions. In this context her general demeanor and symptoms vastly improved. The fact that she could play out these feelings on the dolls, with me, and that her mother and other family members survived intact after these sessions, seemed to be liberating.

Gradually she became bolder, indicating that one of the dolls was to be me and then attacking it, carefully watching for my reactions. My survival of her expressions of murderous feelings and my lack of anger or withdrawal seemed to impress her. In fact, I encouraged her and told her I was pleased she could feel brave enough to do this. I also emphasized the difference between wishes, play acting, and actions in reality. I noted that killing me in play could not kill me in reality or even alienate me. And I emphasized this was true in relation to her mother and her family as well, relating explicitly to what I sensed to be her fears about her own possible responsibility for her mother's illness.

The culmination of all this work was a dramatic increase in her ability to truly "play." She actually began to be playful with me. She would start to tell me about her life at home and at the same time make a point of keeping secrets from me. I acknowledged that there was no way I could read her mind or know her feelings unless she chose to tell me. She delighted in this affirmation of our separateness. This culminated in lively games of peek-a-boo and the first expressions of real laughter and expansiveness.

Our sessions were now joyful and exhilarating, as she engaged in water play and began painting, climbing, jumping and using everything in the room in the service of "pretending." She initiated games of throwing and catching. Eventually checkers and marbles were flying over and under the desk and the room was filled with laughter and excitement. She also began to put on a toy stethoscope and to tell me I was she and she was me, showing she could play at "confusion" without getting confused. She began to joke and play tricks on me, and to jump and to run. It was clear that she could "touch" without fear at this point, and could move out into space without fear of destroying either herself or me or being destroyed.

A new pattern then emerged in which she would generally order me around, telling me "Do this!" "Do that!" "Get this!" "Get that!" I obeyed, to her delight, as she experimented with "using" me in these ways.

By the time we terminated she was a bright, lively, and extremely engaging little girl.

Using countertransference in the ways I have described inevitably structures a much more personal kind of engagement than might occur otherwise. The impact of this cannot be overlooked. The patient is confronted with the analyst as a human being, with sensitivities, vulnerabilities, and limitations. This allows the patient to recognize the necessity for his or her own active collaboration. The unique kind of intimacy that is so structured has effects beyond the content of what is exchanged; these effects must be explored in what becomes an endless progression that continues to open on itself, often in very exciting and lively ways.

The emphasis is on process and experience, not on content, as instead of feeling limited by our subjectivity and trying to defend against it we begin to use it as a powerful source of data and as a basis for opening a unique kind of analytic exploration that can lead to places neither patient or analyst could have predicted beforehand and which neither could possibly have reached alone.

CHAPTER 8

Playfulness

MY FOCUS IN THIS CHAPTER will be on some of the ways in which playfulness can be of value in the establishment, maintenance, and advancement of a viable analytic process, as well as on the ways it can serve as a measure of analytic achievement.

There is a growing body of data documenting the fact that, in order to keep the work alive and vital or even to establish an analytic relationship, especially with more disturbed patients, there are times when the analyst must be innovative and creative. Playfulness can be useful toward this end; indeed it is an underused medium, the potential value of which may not be fully appreciated.

Winnicott (1971), for example, writes that playing is more than simply helpful. He states that it is essential to the analytic experience, remarking, "It is in playing and only in playing that the individual child or adult is able to be creative and to use the whole personality, and it is only in being creative that the individual discovers the self" (p. 54).

He elaborates that *playing has to be spontaneous and not compliant or acquiescent,* if psychotherapy is to be done" (p. 51, italics in original), and that there is a kind of magic in play and playfulness, but a magic that is precarious, since "playing is always liable to become frightening" (p. 50).

Therefore, he emphasizes, "Games and their organization must be looked upon as part of an attempt to forestall the frightening aspect of playing" (p. 50).

Winnicott comments that *"psychotherapy is done in the overlap of the two play areas, that of the patient and that of the therapist.* If the therapist cannot play, then he is not suitable for the work. If the patient cannot play, then something needs to be done to enable the patient to become able to play, after which psychotherapy may begin. The reason why playing is essential is that it is in playing that the patient is being creative" (p. 54, italics in original).

Play may be a "prelude," he notes, to more intensive effort in that the patient may be ready for analysis only *"after* experiencing the understanding" during play and that possibility for "communication at a deep level" which this kind of interaction provides.

Winnicott presents us with a paradox. According to him play is the actual medium of self-discovery and thereby of analytic effort. If the patient has difficulties in being able to play, the first task of treatment is to achieve the ability to play, so analysis can begin. Yet this must be accomplished analytically. Winnicott apparently uses the term "play" to encompass all the varying modes that contribute to the analytic process.

Bateson (1972), an anthropologist, affirming the similarity of the process of therapy and the phenomenon of play, states that paradoxes, such as those involved in play, "are a necessary ingredient in that process of change which we call psychotherapy."

He explains:

As we see it, the process of psychotherapy is a framed interaction between two persons in which the rules are implicit but subject to change. Such change can only be proposed by experimental action, but every such experimental action, in which a proposal to change the rules is implicit, is itself a part of the ongoing game. It is this combination of logical types within the single meaningful act that gives to therapy the character not of a rigid game like canasta, but instead that of an evolving system of interaction. (p. 192)

Bateson emphasizes that "human verbal communication can operate and always does operate at many contrasting levels of abstraction." He points out that a very important stage in the evolution of communicative capacity occurs when the individual ceases to respond automatically to the communications of another. In playfulness the words used do not stand for what they literally mean, and paradox is often a critical element. Bateson states that the capacity to participate playfully "marks a step forward in the evolution of communication." It can serve as a form of metacommunication, in which the subject of the communication is the relationship of the speakers.

In the kind of playful interactions I consider here my emphasis is on the mutual experience of fun and pleasure. The capacity for this kind of playfulness can evolve in any of a number of ways. Sometimes it requires years of serious and painstaking analytic work.

Playfulness can include the use of humor and irony, affectionate kinds of teasing, banter and repartee, joint fantasy, and a host of other possibilities. Because it can effectively communicate on multiple levels simultaneously and allow for transcending communicative barriers, play can cut through distance and expand the range of communication. It can even serve to restructure the relationship or the focus of the interaction, by calling attention to interactive and relational considerations. In essence, it can be catalytic in enabling the patient to have a new experience in relation to himself or herself or a new experience of intimacy in relation to another. It can become a basis for experimentation and exploration, as it provides an opportunity to rediscover and integrate disavowed or repudiated aspects of self. It can also allow for the discovery of undeveloped resources. At times the value of playfulness lies precisely in the kind of affective experience it may help generate and the opportunity this provides for the patient to discover this potential in himself or herself.

In some instances the realization that positive affective connection is possible is the most profound insight that emerges. Some patients learn that they have a capacity for tenderness and affection, or for humor and wit, which heretofore had never been expressed. Some discover their ability to deal with frustration or disappointment. These experiences of self-discovery can become a source of pride and expanding self-esteem.

One patient described the impact of our mutual pleasure in an interaction as follows: Although she had always assumed she was insatiable, a bottomless pit of desire, and was afraid to want for fear that there would be no way to limit her craving, our playful interaction gave her an opportunity to discover how *"satisfied"* she could be as she experienced my pleasure in relation to her. Her fear had been that she would want to be with me twenty-four hours a day, that I would find this distasteful, and that she would be unable to tolerate the frustration of having to deal with the fact that it was self-evident this could not be. Our playful exchanges, and the genuine mutual satisfaction they provided, allowed her to discover that she was indeed able to tolerate frustration and accept the limitations of our relationship.

On reading this she elaborated that the playful encounter gave her a whole new perspective.

"It wasn't just that we could have a good time together; it was that something from deep inside me could be communicated to you and could reach something that was deep inside you that had a mixture of sadness and good feeling. I felt we gave each other something by having that moment. It thus was also that something painful could be expressed and had a certain sweetness that came from being able to share it. It definitely was a moment where I didn't feel alone. I had my experience and you had your experience and they weren't exactly the same but there was something for each of us that connected us to each other. When I try to tap these kinds of feelings by myself I only feel alone and only feel the pain I don't feel that other tender feeling, the feeling of being held and of some comfort. But not only that, it also has some sense of self-regard. I respect my feelings more. It's the joy of being able to communicate. That was the playful part for me. That is why it felt satisfying and not just needy."

I distinguish spontaneous kinds of playfulness, which involve the mutual experience of fun and pleasure, from other forms, and uses of play. For example, during Winnicott's squiggle game (1971), in which each person draws a line, or scribble, in turn, so that both create a story or picture together, the playful engagement is relatively structured; though it can become playful in the way I am considering, it does not always. I also distinguish it from forms of hostility or denigration in the guise of humor or playfulness, which may involve negative, detached, or contemptuous feelings, and which can be injurious. In the kind of interaction I describe, the affective experiences that evolve in the interaction are often critical.

Sometimes the realization of the possibility of positive, even joyful, relatedness may become the point at which a patient can begin to recognize and acknowledge painful aspects of former experiences, or of his or her own behavior or character, with which he or she may never have been able to deal. When this occurs it often allows the patient, finally, to begin a needed process of mourning.

Working playfully requires spontaneity and means trusting one's intuitive clinical sensibility before it can be consciously thought through. Although it is not calculated or premeditated, this does not mean that it is not informed by one's clinical expertise. On the contrary, even as decisions to be playful sometimes may precede rather than follow more conscious kinds of logical consideration, they involve complex clinical judgments. The question becomes: Do we think a particular response will be technically facilitating? rather than: Do we understand exactly what is going on with the patient, the treatment or ourselves, at any given moment? Heimann's (1950) observation that the analyst's unconscious is always ahead of his or her conscious in relation to the patient seems relevant. I think it is this level of our own experience that we actually draw upon when we make a decision to intervene playfully.

In considering the varying forms playfulness can take in the analytic situation, it is useful to distinguish between playfulness initiated by the patient and playfulness initiated by the analyst.

Patients' expressions of playfulness are obviously subject to analytic exploration, as would be any other kind of patient expression. They can be a means of testing the boundaries of the relationship, the limits of one's power and of one's ability to have an impact on the analyst; or they may be expressions of affection or warmth, even an experiment with tenderness.

With some patients, apparent playfulness can be defensive, calculated, even driven. It may be a means to be seductive and disarming. Or it may mask hostility. Certainly, when playfulness is used to manipulate and control, failure to identify this or going along with the patient's pseudo-playfulness can become a form of collusion, a way of avoiding the analytic process. Nevertheless, there are times when being able to join the patient in his or her playfulness and to be responsive to the patient's playful overture can be the most analytically facilitating response of all, and when failure to do so can be a form of resistance, a measure of the analyst's rigidity and lack of imagination. In some instances it may mask the analyst's fear of engaging his or her own spontaneous experience and/or the potential intimacy of the moment.

Playfulness initiated by the analyst is much more complex. Obviously, there are dangers of seduction, manipulation, even coercion, or of what Stern (1985) calls "misattunement" and "emotional theft." This can only reinforce cynicism, despair, and defensiveness.

At any given moment the analyst cannot know whether responding playfully will expand or impede analysis or whether his or her impulses to become playful reflect some kind of self-indulgent, countertransferential response, or an astute, intuitive form of response to a communication from the patient, of which neither patient nor analyst may be consciously aware.

Similarly, though the achievement of a capacity for playfulness in some treatments in which negative feelings have prevailed is usually a positive development, in other contexts one could question whether it might limit the potential for the unfolding of negative feelings.

The analyst's playfulness surely can be experienced as some form of sexual teasing or some kind of untoward provocation, and may evoke hostility; alternatively it may be a countertransferential enactment and/or a way of protecting oneself from the intimacy of the moment rather than a way of developing it.

Nevertheless, these concerns can be raised with regard to the most standard kinds of analyst participation as well, including the most seemingly serious and thoughtful. They can also be raised with regard to the analyst's use of silence.

For these reasons it is clear that avoiding playfulness does not preclude dangers of mystification, seduction, coercion, or manipulation, or of transference cure. To do so requires that the analyst monitor the impact of his or her participation, whatever form it may take, in an ongoing way (Levenson, 1972, 1983; Ehrenberg, 1974, 1982a, 1984a; Feiner, 1979, 1983; Gill, 1983, 1984; Hoffman, 1983). At times the very process of monitoring this impact, and of monitoring the repercussions of the monitoring, which has effects as well, can become the heart of the work.

Fromm-Reichmann (1950, 1952), Tower (1956), Winnicott (1956), and Levenson (1972, 1983), among others, have emphasized that even negative analytic developments can constitute analytic opportunities leading to productive outcomes if followed through with analytic care and diligence. I emphasize this not to imply that this gives one license to intervene playfully in thoughtless or impulsive ways, with the idea that one can always work one's way out of chaos, but because playfulness, which may be the most effective way to make a point, requires us to seize the moment or to forfeit it altogether.

Even in those instances in which I have playfully teased someone and it turned out to have been a "mistake" in the sense that the patient took my comment in some untoward way, I have found that it was useful for both of us to be able to explore the entire experience.

Addressing something playfully can be a way to convey the message that no matter how problematic or painful a situation may be it is not necessarily tragic, and that the analyst assumes it is something analyst and patient have the resources to deal with. For example, it can convey the message, which might not otherwise be heard, *"I think you underestimate who you are and what you have to offer."*

This can spark curiosity, hope, and even wonder: *"What is it that I don't see about myself and why?"* Or playfulness can convey the message, *"I can see your faults and limitations and still appreciate your capabilities."* This is particularly relevant if the patient has difficulties dealing with ambivalence and tends to feel rejecting when he or she experiences negative feelings or is critical of self or other, or if he or she tends to engage in denial or resort to manic defenses. Although this obviously can be addressed in any number of analytic ways, the communication from the analyst that it is possible to face the negative in oneself or in the other without rejecting the total person or losing sight of the positive may open a whole new perspective. This may be necessary to enable the patient to deal with the full scope of his or her experience.

With patients whose treatment is characterized by morbidity and humorlessness, as well as by repetitive dissatisfaction and anger in relation to the analyst, a playful challenge at an opportune moment in the face of the patient's dour gloom and doom can be quite disarming and reassuring. It can help keep the issues life size, rather than letting them escalate to unrealistic, even terrifying, proportions.

For some playfulness can provide a sense of relief, as it establishes that it is possible to open oneself without anticipating rejection, humiliation, attack or blame. It can also be a means to help the patient become aware of his or her tendencies to be self-critical. Playfulness may make it possible to establish an emotional context secure enough for abandonment of even the most paranoid attitudes.

As their capacity for playfulness has developed some extremely paranoid patients have described their pride in being able to "hang in" at times when formerly they might have "freaked out," literally run from the room, or withdrawn from the relationship with hurt and/or hate. Sensitivities that might have made the work problematic for weeks or months were resolved in one or two sessions with the analyst's appropriately playful response.

One patient who typically would have reacted with paranoid rage was actually able to laugh as she was presented with the untenability of the bind she was creating when she indicated that she would be furious if I said anything to push her one way or another, and yet would be equally angry if I didn't tell her what to do.

Sometimes playful engagement has served to facilitate insights about how threatened the patient may have been by emergent erotic or affectionate feelings toward the analyst. In these situations playful experiences have helped to demonstrate that the need to attack or denigrate the analyst reflected a desperate effort to ward off the threat of positive affect. One patient reported becoming aware of how she invariably came to hate many of the people she cared most about precisely because her caring made her so vulnerable to disappointment or betrayal. There was even a sense of feeling violated when she did care. It was as though the other had somehow seduced her into caring against her will and that she had been emotionally raped.

Playful encounters permit the boundaries and structure of a relationship to be challenged. They can serve as an important medium for working through, as they provide the opportunity for the patient to test the limits of his or her fantasied omnipotence and/or fragility. Being able to be playful, even irreverent, in the face of a patient's anger or despair is a way of communicating one's refusal to be intimidated or to give up no matter how difficult the situation. It establishes, within the actual two-person interaction, the limits of the patient's omnipotence and the strength of the analyst's ability to stay alive despite the patient's efforts to the contrary. In this kind of interactive encounter, it is this evidence of the analyst's autonomy and commitment, not the specific content of the words, that may be most significant. And although this has to be addressed explicitly after the fact to maintain analytic integrity, the critical point is that a simple verbal exploration would not have the same power.

The opportunity for the patient to discover, in the actual interaction, that both patient and analyst can survive the patient's explorations in self-expression can establish a unique context of safety in which he or she can begin to confront fears and to discover ways in which these may be arbitrary and stifling. In some instances playful engagement can make it more manageable for the patient to explore what the anticipated dangers of closeness might be. Fears of closeness based on fantasies that such feelings open one to the threat of being cannibalized, consumed, violated or betrayed — or even to masochistic wishes for these, including denigration or defilation — often can be explored.

Some patients have stated that the kind of positive feelings they experience in playful interactions are so intense that they fear that, if the relationship were to be threatened or changed in any way, they would become so angry due to their frustration and disappointment that they might lose control, becoming homicidal toward me or suicidal. For such patients, for whom negative feelings often serve as a form of protective insularity, and for whom love is felt to be more threatening than hate, being able to experience and survive positive feelings in the analytic context, along with the sense of vulnerability these feelings generate, can be critical.

With those patients for whom the threat of invasiveness and intrusiveness is always present, playfulness can render such anxieties accessible and provide an opportunity for the patient to discover that there are ways one can open and enrich oneself by exercising choices. Playful engagement can facilitate a collaborative exploration of the complex boundary confusions with which they may be struggling, as well as their own contributions in perpetuating them. Particularly at moments of acute vulnerability, when a conventional clinical response might be too ambiguous and lend itself to being interpreted as cold and rejecting, a playful response can be extremely reassuring in establishing that it is possible to explore certain issues without fear of rejection or humiliation. It can also be a means to help the patient become aware of his or her tendencies to be self-critical, judgmental, or self-righteous, or to project these qualities onto another.

In some instances I have found that my use of affectionate teasing has served to expose a patient's inability to respond to this kind of communication except literally. In effect, it helped to reveal the degree of anxiety that can be aroused when the patient is faced with certain kinds of ambiguity and/or the potential for certain kinds of emotion.

Similarly, with patients who seem to be very bright and sophisticated, and who might be quite comfortable in initiating playful action, the analyst's playfulness can be useful in revealing their inability to deal with playfulness initiated by another, and a tendency to become concrete in response, which may not otherwise become apparent. This can help to illuminate profound fears and/or conflicts and allow these to be worked through in the analytic relationship. In such contexts, the development of the capacity for responsiveness to the analyst's playfulness often constitutes a measure of the achievement of the ability to engage in more complex kinds of abstract communication and metacommunication.

Generally, when playfulness is threatening there is a history of danger in playful or close relationships. Experiences within the analytic situation can help reveal ways in which patients may have felt seduced – then betrayed – in playful interactions with parental figures.

Obviously, there are times when playfulness would be inappropriate and counterproductive, and when playful intervention could preclude a necessary experience of rage, depression, or anxiety. Nevertheless, even in the context of negative feelings, there are instances when playfulness can be useful. When analytic work seems to be deadlocked, or when achieving an analytic engagement seems impossible, I have sometimes had an impulse to "liven things up." Since this does not always occur to me in such contexts, and in many instances I would consider it egregiously inappropriate, when it does occur it seems to reflect the fact that I am tuning into something. And although sometimes clarifying this in my own mind may be sufficient, at other moments I might decide to actually respond in a playful way. And, despite my concern that in doing so I might be engaging in some form of countertransferential enactment or exploitative self-indulgence of which I may not yet be aware, these interventions usually serve to set the analytic process in motion. Once this occurs it is possible to explore what the impact of my participation has been, what might have been going on earlier, and what the transference-countertransference issues might be.

PAULA

As I noted in Chapter 2, in the early phase of my work with Paula, who was suffering from a postpartum depression, she was able to verbalize only minimally and at times was unable to sit still in the consulting room. She usually arrived late for sessions and left early, sometimes after only a few minutes; sometimes she wouldn't show up at all. At times while she was there she might pace back and forth. Once she actually began banging on and kicking the doors in my office.

I emphasize the tension, and the level of aggressive feelings that dominated the early period of our work together, to make clear that our later being able to engage in the playful, sometimes silly interactions I will now describe, and to experience and express positive feelings, was no small analytic achievement. In a sense it must be viewed as the fruit of the very painstaking analytic work that preceded it.

Much later in this treatment, in the context of an atmosphere of increasing freedom and intimacy, Paula openly acknowledged how strong her feelings for me had become. Yet she also expressed some skepticism. She wanted to know what I felt for her. Was she just another "case"? It clearly mattered to her to know that I took our relationship seriously. This culminated in a moving expression of how vulnerable she now felt. Following this she began to joke that even if we both saw each other as *"beautiful, wonderful people"* it might be a *"folie à deux." "What if we are fooling ourselves and each other?"*

When I replied that I thought there was no requirement that we be either beautiful or wonderful for either of us to care about the other, this seemed to touch her. She then got up and began to pace, as she described how much she loved her daughter, and how vulnerable she felt to care so much, obviously referring to our relationship as well. Being able to experience, express, and survive such feelings seemed to be healing.

One scenario we both later enjoyed evolved during a session in which she seemed restless and began pacing back and forth. After a while I got up and moved into her chair, which surprised her. At this point she sat in my chair. When the buzzer signaling the next patient sounded, she asked whether she could press the return buzzer. I said yes and she did so with excitement. Then the phone rang and she asked whether she should answer the phone. When I said "No!" we both laughed. Following this interaction we were able to talk about some of the boundary issues, and what they meant to her, in a way that had not been possible earlier.

Later in our work Paula began to take great pleasure in relating to me all the gory details of the horror stories she loved to read. She was immensely delighted with what she experienced as her ability to shock and horrify me. She teased me about her perception that I only read "good books" and was so "straight." As she made a point of emphasizing the ways in which we were different, we were able to begin to explore her concerns about maintaining her identity and the degree to which she struggled with fears that being like me in any way threatened her sense of her own integrity. What became clear was the degree to which these fears prevented her from being able to define herself in her own terms. This period of our work led eventually to a moment, sometime later, when she poignantly expressed her sadness about only reading *"Martian horror books,"* and commented that she wanted to *"go to the library and read all the classics I never read, poetry and everything."*

In fact, as she began to report feeling freer to be either the same or different from me, or anyone, depending on her own preferences and abilities, this stimulated a train of associations to an earlier struggle with her concerns about sameness and difference in relation to her parents as well, and to the fact that there had been a time in her life when she had loved to read serious writers. She noted that she was now beginning to wonder why she had stopped.

As our work progressed her dreams began to shift in the direction of becoming less gory, and sometimes were even actually positive in feeling. In this context, on one occasion she reported a dream in which she was on the ocean liner, the QE II. She had apparently walked into a place she was not supposed to be. The captain confiscated her suitcase and proceeded to cut the sleeves off her best dress as some kind of punishment. She remarked how amazing it was that he was only attacking her dress and not her, in contrast to her earlier dreams. I acknowledged the importance of this; yet I also challenged playfully that she was still being victimized. Why had she not fought back, even hit him below the belt? This idea excited her enormously and led to much laughter. I deliberately had not addressed the extremely complex transferential issues directly, instead choosing to work playfully within her metaphors and to emphasize options she was not aware of, because I felt that would be most useful at this juncture.[10]

When, sometime later, she reported a sense of how much she felt herself changing, even though she couldn't exactly explain how or why, she noted that what was striking was her realization that although she had always expressed a fear that if she were to change she might "lose herself," she now was excited to discover instead that she was beginning to "find herself" more and more.

In this context she reported, *"An image comes to mind — 'I am a shadow of my former self' — but I have never been that yet, that's my goal. I feel I am a shadow of the fledgling real me."* Over time, as she began to come even closer to that "real me" than she had ever been before, she reported with excitement an image of *"a zipper opening on my throat and singing birds come flying out!"*

She contrasted her current sense of well-being to the initial period of our relationship, in which she had been pacing back and forth in my office and banging on the doors and walls in a state of extreme agitation, and she elaborated a dream she remembered from that early period in which *"Your office was filled with heads, like trophies, people's heads, stuffed. And there was dried shed skin. That is your job, isn't it? People come here and shed their skin. I don't know if the mounted heads was what I thought your attitude was. But it was pretty grisly in here, I tell you!"* Sometime later she revealed that in contrast to the image of the singing birds she had reported so recently, at that time she had felt *"like a giant blue bird, with white underfeathers, batting around the room, smashing against the walls, with feathers flying all over."*

By this time Paula reported a growing sense of pride about the fact that her relationships with both her husband and her child had become very satisfying and important to her, and that this was true with regard to our relationship as well. She also reported that, although it had not been easy, she had been successful in her effort to give up drugs and alcohol.

It may be no surprise that Paula never became a woman of many words during the six years of our work together. Nevertheless, in contrast to her earlier fears that she would lose herself by putting things into words, and having things *"leak out of me like a puddle,"* and in contrast to fears expressed in a later phase of our work of putting things into the *"wrong words,"* with the risk that this might become a way of *"closing off something forever—forever sealing it off,"* Paula began to play with words and to have great fun doing so. At times she was so clever and funny that she actually amazed herself. She demonstrated an ability to be incisive, penetrating, sometimes even cutting, all in her own remarkably terse way. Our sessions came to be characterized by so much laughter that eventually I began to feel guilty for getting paid for having so much fun. When I raised my concerns about the usefulness of our continuing to spend our time simply having fun, she let me know her disappointment that I did not appreciate the degree to which this continued to be an experience of self-discovery for her. She stated that because she still had moments in which she experienced herself as "fragmented " and "alien" in almost every other context, it meant a great deal to her to feel that we could continue to make contact with each other and have so much fun together. In her words, the fact that *"someone like you could really enjoy being with me and have fun with me allows me to feel whole and human."* I of course learned a great deal from Paula in that moment.

Paula had a second child during the course of our work. Although this was not without experiences of intense strain and anxiety, particularly during the second pregnancy experience, she was able to contain these feelings, and neither they nor the subsequent birth of her child interfered with her relationship with her daughter or with her husband. When the new baby was born she did not have a postpartum depression and was able to delight in and care for both children. She eventually also began to explore ways of developing and pursuing her own interest in singing.

Michael

Michael began treatment in a state of anxiety and was very tense in our early sessions as he elaborated gory fantasies of being mutilated or castrated by razor blades (see Chapter 7). These fantasies frightened him and led him to wonder whether he might be "crazy." During this period I painstakingly tried to track the details of subtle aspects of what went on between us, so as to determine what triggered these reactions. We were able to determine that these might occur at moments when he noticed me looking at the clock. In such instances he did not experience anger, or rage, or hurt, but rather would experience a razor blade fantasy, usually with himself as the victim. In one instance, described in Chapter 7, he actually experienced a frightening loss of touch with reality after I had canceled a session unexpectedly. Only after we dealt with this in our immediate interaction, and he was able to recognize how angry and hurt he was in response to this cancellation, was he able to regain his grasp on the situation.

In contrast to the tension and anxiety that had characterized our earlier work, in the period of work I will describe now our sessions began to be a pleasure for both of us, as he began to enjoy flaunting his intelligence and creativity and to challenge and compete with me in a playful way. In one session he dared me to read my notes back to him and expressed surprise and delight when I did so. At that point he told me to be sure to write down that I was doing so. The playfulness became a medium for experiments in assertiveness. It seemed obvious to me that he was using our relationship as a testing ground.

These playful efforts became self-reinforcing and led to bolder kinds of playful expression. He became overtly seductive, vigorously challenging the boundaries of our relationship, as he began to describe fantasies about a romance between us. He would elaborate detailed fantasies of our running away together to exotic and wonderful places, and he began to enjoy being able to play with such a fantasy. At other moments he offered himself to be adopted as my child, asking if I would be more receptive to that. He promised to be well behaved if I would agree to take him into my home, and argued that, since we got along so well, why should he have to look for someone else to be involved with at all. He was charming and funny and our sessions were fun for both of us. However, even as he played with these fantasies, the fantasies established as much distance as they did closeness. If I became too playful in response, the actual closeness this seemed to establish aroused fantasies of his being murdered or castrated, which we explored.

Eventually he was able to articulate his fear of what might happen if he were to dare to be less than charming, and in this context some of the old razor blade fantasies began to reappear. Sometimes, however, he would have a totally new kind of fantasy, in which his aggression was specifically directed at me. Although the content was murderous and frightening, as he realized they did not seem to pose a real threat to either of us or to our relationship he began to be less frightened by his own aggressive impulses. Eventually, he even began to be able to enjoy his own aggressive fantasies and to develop these in very playful ways. For instance, he seemed to delight himself as he developed one fantasy that involved a cartoonlike scenario of getting rid of me by having the floor around my chair sawed through so that I and my chair would fall to the apartment below.

As we now scrutinized all that was involved, he began to speak more directly about his feelings of vulnerability. He was able to describe his anxieties about getting involved in a sexual way with any woman. These included a phobia of having anyone see his naked body, anxieties about his physical attractiveness and his sexual capacities, and anxieties about being castrated or even murdered. There were associations to specific experiences of hurt and betrayal in relationships with his parents and siblings. He reported that he was amazed to be able to share all of this with me, and he voiced concern about whether I would be jealous if he were ever this free with anyone else. This led to a realization of a wish that I should be, and a fear of what it might mean if I were.

As all this became clarified he reported with surprise that he was aware of feeling more self-confident outside of treatment. In his work he began to be much more productive and assertive and to establish himself as someone of unusual talent and competence. And in his personal life, despite a long-term preoccupation that he might be homosexual, he began to date and to become sexually involved with a young woman. He actually looked physically different, as he stood straighter and taller.

JEFF

Another patient, Jeff (see Chapter 7), seemed solely concerned with charming me. His ingratiating smiles and jokes made me quite uncomfortable and actually had the opposite effect. His alleged playfulness seemed to be calculated and driven. Indeed, I felt a hostile edge to it all. For him, being funny was work, not play, indicating that he needed to stay in control.

What became clear eventually was his cynicism about what treatment could accomplish (he had had prior experiences) and his despair about life and relationships in general. Being charming was a way of insulating himself from treatment and from life. His pseudo-play was actually a formidable defense against a meaningful engagement in any arena. In treatment, in particular, it protected him from being disappointed or helped, both of which were terrifying possibilities. As all this emerged there were some surprising moments in which he was able to experience and acknowledge feelings he had never felt consciously before. These included his terror of feeling vulnerable and inadequate.

The result was that he suddenly began to behave toward me more deferentially than usual, indicating that I had "won" some kind of battle. When I questioned this he revealed that in his relationships in general he was either a "tyrant" or a "wimp" and that he didn't really have any sense of alternative ways of relating. I stressed that I had no interest in getting him to submit to me and that I had hoped our relationship could involve collaborative exploration.

Following this he became extremely self-conscious about the kind of manipulativeness he had formerly engaged in, and very slowly the character of our exchanges began to shift in the direction of a much more mutual kind of repartee. Now, when some of the old tendencies to structure a power struggle were evident, that became something we could joke about.

One scenario followed a very moving session in which he had actually cried, acknowledging the magnitude of his problems, which he had never before fully grasped. It went as follows:

He was my first patient of the day. He came in and commented, not atypically, about the mess of papers near my chair and the disarray of my desk, in a teasing but affectionate way. Then he made some reference to something related to his business, which put him in touch with people of relative prominence. I did not recognize a name he mentioned and he went into a lengthy teasing elaboration of who this person was, emphasizing that he was now enlightening me and broadening my education. Then he began to comment on how sleepy I looked, and asked snidely, *"Is it too early in the day for you to be working?"* sarcastically adding that he surely did not want to impose himself on me if I was too tired.

I found myself yawning increasingly and feeling so sleepy I began to worry that I might actually fall asleep during the session. He noted my facial expression as I struggled to keep my eyes open. I apologized for being so tired. I silently wondered how I would ever get through the day.

At the end of the session he again made some snide remarks, this time about it having been an unproductive session. I replied, somewhat defensively, *"We will have to see—sometimes you can't tell until later."*

When my next patient arrived I was amazed to discover that, despite feeling tired, I had no trouble staying awake and was able to participate with no difficulty. At that point I began to wonder what exactly had been going on in the prior session with Jeff. It was now clear to me that what I had experienced as my own real physical tiredness was not the key to what had occurred.

The next day I described to Jeff how intrigued I now was by the fact that, although I had been so "sleepy" with him, I was wide awake in the session following. I felt it was important that we attempt to understand what had been going on between us. Yes, I had been sleepy, but what had his role been? As I pursued this with him I was as playful as he had been the day before. I asked him whether putting the spotlight on me had been a way of getting it off of himself. Had that been his intention? His response was fascinating. As I focused on him in this way he began to squirm very markedly and to yawn repeatedly and to become increasingly "sleepy." I noted this and playfully confronted him with the fact that, although his effort to "educate" me yesterday had been with regard to my fund of factual knowledge, it seemed what I had learned instead was how to have the same effect on him now as he had managed to have on me then.

We both began to laugh. At this point we were noticeably awake and engaged. What we were able to see at this point was that the previous session actually seemed to reflect a reaction to the session prior, in which he had had the emotional realization about the magnitude of his problems. He now stated that this had felt somewhat humiliating to him. The suggestion was that his effort to put me down in the next hour was a reaction to the pain he had felt in response to that prior session, and that his attempt at playfulness was actually in the service of avoiding the earlier intimacy. It was now possible to engage his fragile sense of self-esteem, his fears of humiliation and of hurt, and his need to stay in control and to assert his power.

As our work progressed he became much more genuinely playful and funny and began to delight in getting me to laugh. Nevertheless, he often would take great pleasure in teasing me once I did begin to laugh, saying that Freud would turn over in his grave if he knew what was going on and that he was sure my colleagues at my institute would be shocked if they were to become aware of how we were spending our sessions. Sometimes I responded to this in kind, wondering out loud how he could determine whether his ability to reduce me to laughter was a measure of his power or whether it indicated I was "easy," a virtual "pushover"? Furthermore, since it was his analysis, who was winning or losing if I didn't fight him and just let myself enjoy the fun? This kind of repartee facilitated engaging his complex feelings about who was in control and raised the question of who was getting the best of whom in our actual interaction, in ways not possible earlier. The fact that we could play with all of this, and talk about it even as we did so, seemed to contribute to a growing sense of intimacy and affection between us and a feeling of knowing each other in a much more direct and incisive way than any revelation of any facts about ourselves might have achieved (see Ehrenberg, 1974).

Jeff began to marvel at the contrast between his awkwardness and self-consciousness in our earlier sessions, as well as his use of pseudo-play to protect himself from getting close, and the kind of intimacy we had now achieved. Ultimately in these mutually playful exchanges he was able to talk about those things he had always assumed to be unshareable. He expressed his pleasure in the realization that I seemed to enjoy our current interactions as much as he did, saying that he had always assumed that no one could possibly find him interesting if he were not being controlling and/or manipulative.

As his capacity to be genuinely playful developed he began to describe with pride a growing ability to distinguish in his own mind between playing the other, as one manipulates a tool or a musical instrument, in the service of one's own agenda (something he considered himself to be a master at and generally was), and the kind of open communication that characterized the more mutual kind of playfulness in which we were now involved. He reported that for the first time he was aware that he no longer felt isolated. And, as he expressed his realization of the joy he felt in the experience of connection, he reported with surprise and with pride the ways in which this seemed to be having repercussions in his relationships outside of treatment. He specifically saw that he had begun to experience a new depth of emotion towards his children, and he actually cried as he articulated this. In this context he began to deal with painful aspects of his past experience which he had never been able to deal with before.

SARA

In one instance, when she was particularly depressed, Sara expressed her concern that I must have regrets about having agreed to work with her, and that she was sure she was my "worst" patient. I found this so absurd that I quipped, quite affectionately, *"No, you are my second to worst patient."* To my surprise she took this quite literally and seemed devastated. Here was an instance where my playfulness certainly did not have the intended effect.

There were several things to consider. Though she had expressed concerns that maintaining our relationship was contingent on her being fun to be with, the facts were that she had been depressed for the first two years of our work, and it was during this period that our relationship had actually developed. It had not been contingent on her being fun to be with at all (see Chapter 4). Was the issue now that I had hooked into her expectation that in any relationship, no matter how positive it may appear, the other person's feelings could change at any moment, and that ultimately she would be subject to rejection or betrayal? Or was she feeling burdened by an idea that she had to be able to function at a level that was difficult for her to sustain in order not to disappoint me? Certainly in expecting her to appreciate my comment as a tease, I was apparently expressing an expectation she was unable to meet. I raised all of this with her.

She responded with associations to particular details of her experience growing up with alcoholic parents, and elaborated that we seemed to be involved in a reenactment of something that she had often gotten into with her mother. These complex issues were now tangibly in evidence and became data for us to work with.

My effort to painstakingly address and clarify all of this seemed to have impact of its own. It seemed that it conveyed to her that I thought we could do so, and that it mattered to me that we should. And it actually began to structure a new experience for her, very different from the one with her mother, as it provided her with an opportunity to realize the extent of her own ability to have an impact on me.

In this specific instance my actual remark, that she was my "second to worst patient," became something she often referred to in the years following. It came to serve as a shared image, a part of the private language that develops in any intimate relationship over time, which encapsulated all that had been involved in that earlier experience. In addition, she used it as a reference point at moments of vulnerability and insecurity or of frustration.

It may be of interest that Sara's response to reading what I have written here was to tell me to be sure to include in my discussion the fact that I was her "second to worst analyst." She also added that she felt her ability to be playful in this way now was a result of our work.

NORA

Nora, who was very bright and psychologically aware, could be quite playful and disarming. It took a long time to realize that any playfulness initiated by me, however, was usually met with suspicion and that she tended to become especially concrete in response, wanting to be very clear of my meaning. Only gradually did I come to realize that anything that threatened to throw her off balance or shake her sense of control, as a playful response initiated by someone else might, seemed to pose a threat.

Once this became clear to me I began to wonder out loud why my playful communications were so problematic for her. And how did she understand her becoming so concrete in response?

She responded with a very complex train of associations, culminating in a description of how she had "made a pact" when a beloved pet had been ill that she would give up something she had wanted very badly at the time if only her pet would get better. Instead the reverse had happened. She ended up getting the thing she had offered to give up and her pet died. On some profound level she then concluded that because she had gotten what she wanted she was responsible for her pet's death.

Articulating this led to associations to the death of her father when she was only three. She was surprised by the intensity of the feelings that now welled up (in fact, she began to cry). Up until that moment she had insisted that her father's death had had no great emotional impact on her because she had been so young at the time. What now emerged was an awareness that on some level she did have concerns about her possible responsibility for her father's death as well.

At this point she was able to talk, with much emotion, about her fears of analysis and of opening herself to her own experience. We were able to recognize how her concreteness actually served to protect herself, and others, from what she feared might be the destructive power of free thoughts or feelings that might emerge in a spontaneous way if she were not in careful control. It was as though she believed that thinking or feeling had life-threatening power.

Ironically, in this instance my playfulness was useful precisely because it helped clarify the fact that, though she could be playful herself, she could not cope with playfulness initiated by another. This allowed us to begin to engage very complex feelings and fears that might have remained extremely elusive otherwise.

I believe that because playfulness can be a serious analytic medium, and at times an extremely penetrating one, the potential benefits of judiciously using playfulness as a means to facilitate and further advance the analytic process, whether initiated by analyst or patient, justify the risks. Furthermore, as this last example illustrates, even when playfulness fails in terms of its intended effect it can still be analytically facilitating.

Some patients who have had previous analysis have tended to be extremely uneasy when I have been playful. Some have even argued that *"this is not analysis."* In such instances it has been particularly moving to me when later they have realized that they have changed in ways they never imagined would have been possible. Ultimately what they question is not my playfulness but rather their former conceptions of what constitutes "analysis."

Playful interactions offer a potential for validation and affirmation, for reducing alienation, for stirring creative aliveness, and for extending the reaches of imagination. They can also become a basis for evolving intimacy and creative engagement, and for experiences of positive, even tender feelings, which may be new for the patient.

This in turn provides an opportunity to deal with the anxieties and fantasies that this kind of intimacy, and the sense of vulnerability it usually involves, may arouse. In some instances playfulness can also be a means to make it possible to deal with negative feelings, even rage, when other kinds of approaches might be ineffective.

In my experience, being able to engage in playful ways in an analytic context, in which the integrity of the relationship is secure, is a means to achieve the kind of personal engagement necessary to stimulate hope, desire, and change.

CHAPTER 9

The Role of Encounter in the Process of Working Through

IN THIS CHAPTER I WILL FOCUS ON the role of encounter in the psychoanalytic process. My view is that in many instances an encounter between patient and analyst is the key to a viable process and the locus of therapeutic action.

By *encounter* I mean those moments in which patient and analyst engage in relatively direct and personal ways. I use the word encounter rather than *confrontation* because confrontation generally tends to imply an adversarial engagement. Encounter, as I define it, can be collaborative and compassionate. It can involve encountering each other's weaknesses as well as strengths; it can involve positive or negative feelings. It can involve attempting to deal with the pulls of transference and countertransference, where these become problematic, or coming to terms with the constraints on both participants necessary to maintain an analytically viable relationship. It can involve transcending artificial restraints that allow for denying or resisting dealing with the personal dimension of the analytic relationship. It can involve dealing with issues of authenticity and of affective absence or presence.

140

My experience is that the moments of relatively intimate and affectively intense engagement that can evolve out of these encounters need not constitute violations of analytic integrity or of neutrality. Rather, to the extent that they can be achieved so that analytic integrity is maintained and preserved, they add a dimension to the work that can be profound and facilitating. If this level of engagement becomes an integral and sustained aspect of the process, it can create a unique context of analytic possibility.

Where the analytic integrity of the work is threatened, an encounter between patient and analyst can become the heart of the work, *as the analyst's insistence on what is incumbent for productive treatment becomes the analytic lever.*

LAURA

I was pregnant when Laura first began treatment but this did not seem to be an issue for her. In the third year of treatment, however, when she learned I was pregnant again, Laura expressed outrage and let loose a torrent of verbal abuse. To "get revenge" she threatened suicide.

When I tried to explore her feelings with her, she only became more abusive. What became clear was that her assumption was that she was not accountable for her behavior because she was "too sick" and that her distress gave her license to threaten me. Apparently, this had been a rationalization for all kinds of interpersonal intimidation tactics throughout her life. I tried to clarify that there was a difference between trying to get revenge and trying to engage in an analytic process. She, in turn, raged that as her analyst I was supposed to accept her behavior no matter what she did. Her view was that since she paid me this gave her certain "rights."

I insisted that this was not an acceptable definition of our relationship as far as I was concerned. I added that unless she took responsibility for her participation in our work she could not blame me if it failed.

She argued strenuously with what I said, but I remained firm, stating that it was necessary and important to explore her hurt and angry feelings but not to enact them. As she became only more abusive, this deteriorated into a shouting match between us and she raged at me for failing her by getting angry. At this point I held firm to my view that her abusiveness was not acceptable, but I conceded that my losing my temper suggested that she might be right—perhaps someone else might be able to work with her more effectively. To my surprise, before I could say more she responded by declaring that it was actually a relief for her to know I could "lose it" too. It allowed her to feel she wasn't the "only bad one" in the room and that therefore she wasn't "alone."

Laura then began to sob as she expressed relief and gratitude that I had stood up to her. She stated that no one had ever related to her in this way before, and she told of fears that, like her parents, I wouldn't be able to "handle" her. This was followed by associations to how she had terrorized her mother with her tantrums when she was a child. She reported that, instead of trying to stop her, her mother had let her become "loathsome" and then hated her for being that way. She continued to sob as she remarked, *"If only she had stopped me!"*

She described how angry she now was that her mother had not stopped her. She then expressed a wish to have control imposed from outside because of her fears of her own destructive potential to herself and to others.

This led to an opportunity to consider that, even if her mother or I had had problems setting limits or had hurt her, advertently or inadvertently, this did not absolve her of her responsibility for her own behavior.

As a result of this very painful period of work, she reported finally understanding the degree to which she actually enjoyed tyrannizing others while presenting herself as the innocent, self-righteous victim. She described with embarrassment the "pleasure," the almost "sexual pleasure," this gave her. And, as she began to realize that she could take responsibility for helping me to understand her, she reported finding that she was actually able to take pleasure and pride in being able to do so.

In the months following she went through a self-conscious and painful exploration of how "outrageous" she had been to me and to her parents over the years. She elaborated how she had walked all over them. Though she was still angry that they had permitted her to do this, she also began to express remorse for having exploited what she began to see with growing compassion as their vulnerability and limitations.

Recognizing this evoked much sadness and pain, but also a sense of relief. As she began increasingly to see herself apart from her mother and to be aware of options she had not quite grasped before, the lines between us became clearer. She began to feel relatively safer and more curious, as opposed to feeling threatened and offensively defensive, and began to engage in a painful period of mourning.

Although at times she expressed much anger at me for being the instrument of her current grief and pain, the result was that our relationship began to be more and more free. Now, rather than getting hopelessly tangled in battles over who was doing what to whom, we began to laugh together when things started to revert to the old patterns. The kinds of struggles that might have gone on over weeks or months in the past were resolved in one or two sessions, as we both felt safer and more trusting.

Although Laura continued to give me a hard time when she was frustrated, deep feelings of affection, tenderness and respect developed between us. In contrast to the long and difficult periods that had been so painful for both of us, our sessions began to be a pleasure. For the first time she began to explore her attachment to me and expressed surprise at the intensity of her feelings about sessions ending, about the time she had to wait between sessions, and about the pain of feeling so "vulnerable."

SARA

Sara became increasingly vulnerable as she became more involved, taking every sign of tiredness or distraction on my part extremely personally. If I were a few minutes late she would feel deeply hurt and betrayed. Even though she had been extremely deferential in the early years of our work, she now would attack me for being unfair to her and for being so uncaring. Her openly expressed anger might be viewed as a sign of some progress; however, the problem now was that she used her experience of feeling hurt as a reason to negate our relationship as having any value or meaning to her.

I responded by letting her know I was sorry if I had hurt her, but also expressed my sense of feeling burdened by her extreme sensitivity. It was almost as though I had begun to feel tyrannized by her vulnerability.

She responded with anger and attacked me, saying that she heard me saying that she was a "bad" person. She insisted that it was my problem and that I was not owning my part in provoking her. To a certain extent she was of course correct. The issue, however, was that this seemed to be precisely what happened when she began to be involved with *anyone* in an intimate way. She was like a raw nerve, hypersensitive and apt to feel endlessly hurt, betrayed, and devastated, as even minor disappointments were experienced as major and insurmountable.

In this context I told her that I could understand how disappointed and frustrated she felt but that I felt it was important to focus on how her taking things so personally and feeling so wounded, and then cutting off so angrily, was really a problem she had to address.

She experienced my comments as yet another attack, and again attacked me for hurting her and for not taking responsibility for my hurting her, using what I had just said as more evidence of her point. We seemed hopelessly locked in this tangle.

When I then noted that some of what was going on between us now seemed to be similar to interactions she had described with her mother, this seemed to sufficiently detoxify the immediate moment to pique her analytic curiosity. She produced associations documenting an awareness of both how tyrannical she could be and how tyrannized she had felt by parents whose drunkenness, indifference, and unpredictability had left her feeling unable to be heard, uncared about, and inevitably, devastatingly betrayed. She reported:

"I never knew when I came home what to expect. You couldn't have anything good, you could only hope and be devastated, until you finally turn the switch off inside you. You just turn the lights off, and that is it.

"Sometimes being tyrannical is a reaction of trying to control something. I guess that is what tyrannical people do. To try to keep

a grip on something so tightly so there are no surprises, no hurt, nothing. It's aggressive desperateness."

She now related this to her quickness to feel obliterated and tyrannized by me, and to the ways she could obliterate and tyrannize me.

Then she revealed, with much emotion, *"My fear is of getting into a sadomasochistic relationship and the other person won't be able to stop it."* She expressed her relief and gratitude that I had not let her play this out between us and had helped to focus it as an issue we could now talk about.

The result of recognizing all of this was that her anger and sense of righteous indignation gave way to sadness and a kind of embarrassment. Her physical appearance actually changed dramatically, as she visibly softened. At this point she was able to acknowledge and engage the issue of her own sense of vulnerability.

Other, more extreme situations come to mind. Some patients describe how sexually arousing it is for them to tell the analyst, in pornographic detail, their sexual fantasies. One spoke of the "charge" that he felt in being able to *"put ideas into your (the analyst's) mind and force you (the analyst) to think about them almost as a symbolic rape and sexual violation."*

For patients whose fantasies revolve around bondage, domination, sadomasochistic exercises in power, the opportunity to tie the analyst up symbolically, to try to torment and frighten him or her, can be extremely exciting and sexually arousing. Some such patients have reported how thrilling it was to realize that by virtue of my role as analyst, I was within the hour, their "captive."

For these patients, who generally prefer an unwilling partner, the analyst's efforts to attempt to analyze what is going on are often experienced as a protest, which only heightens their excitement. If listening to and/or analyzing of what is going on are experienced by the patient as sexually stimulating, the analyst's technical dilemma is obvious.

In one such instance, when I told a patient that if he were looking for sexual or sadomasochistic thrills he could get more satisfaction for less money elsewhere, he responded with the admission that he had been testing me. He stated that he had assumed that I would not be willing to work with him if I knew what his fantasies and impulses really were, and/or that I would not be strong enough to handle what might emerge. My response had thus signaled to him a possibility in treatment he had not anticipated.

This patient, who had delighted in viewing me as his captive within the hours now reported realizing for the first time that *he* was the one who was really the captive, captive of his need to keep structuring sadomasochistic sexualized interactions. He revealed the sense of torment, shame, and humiliation he now felt realizing this. As he penetrated this internal barrier he produced detailed associations to painful childhood experiences of having been beaten, which he had never talked of before. He also described feeling acutely in touch with the feelings of terror, humiliation, and helpless rage that he had experienced then.

With other patients, who have attempted to terrorize me with fantasies of harming my children as well as me, or by describing cases where other analysts had been attacked or even murdered by patients, all while emphasizing their own fears of losing control and becoming violent, my saying that I could not continue to work if I was being terrorized (which was not a ploy but a genuine response) evoked reactions I could not have anticipated. One of these patients expressed his surprise at being able to have such impact. He then reported, with much emotion, that the fact that I did not immediately throw him out, and seemed to feel it still might be possible to work together, helped him to realize that he had some choice about how he was to behave, no matter what his feelings were. At that point he reported an insight: he had been acting towards me in much the same way as a man who had sexually abused him as a child had acted towards him. For the first time he realized this was not necessarily who he was or wanted to be. This interaction marked a turning point in that treatment.

By establishing that there is a difference between an associative process in which the patient is pursuing an analytic goal and the kinds of verbalizations that are intended to hurt, abuse, seduce, manipulate, coerce, or even to placate or to please, and then stating that we may be open to one kind of relationship but not the other, we confront the patient with the need to make a choice.

Expecting the patient to take responsibility for his or her participation makes it possible to explore difficulties and resistances to assuming an active, responsible role in the analytic undertaking. In this way an internal struggle can be experienced and engaged, rather than allowed to be externalized and played out interactively. Even where this may be painful, it is integrative, as the patient is helped to recognize the complexity of his or her own experience and the impossibility of avoiding making choices, since not choosing is a choice itself.

The key here is to be able to attend simultaneously to health and pathology, to positive and negative, and to the adult and the child in the patient. This allows us to convey the message that the analyst believes the patient has the capacity to function in her or his own behalf (Fromm-Reichmann, 1950) and to provide opportunities for patients to discover unknown resources in themselves.

In contrast, even in the context of the severest pathology, not holding the patient responsible and accountable for her or his behavior and participation is patronizing and can be undermining. In addition, if the analyst can be coerced, co-opted, intimidated, or simply rendered ineffectual, not only is the therapeutic potential foreclosed, but the experience can become terrifying. It can confirm the patient's worst fears and may be experienced, even if not consciously so, as the ultimate form of rejection and abandonment. This can lead to dangerous acting out, even suicide, often without patient or analyst understanding the degree to which the patient's acting out is a direct response to the analyst's impotence, detachment, or silence.

Bird (1972), echoing a point made by Winnicott (1949), emphasizes that there are times when:

> our not confronting the patient becomes in itself not merely
> an unfriendly act but a destructive one. By not confronting
> the patient with the actuality of the patient's secret, silent
> obstruction of analytic progress, the analyst himself silently
> introduces even greater obstructions. (p. 294)[11]

I believe that the analyst's ability to confront destructive use of the relationship, particularly where the analyst's failure represents a perverse kind of triumph for the patient, may be essential to restore or establish a viable analytic process. It may be the only way to establish one's *neutrality* and one's commitment to maintaining analytic integrity. Nevertheless, how we engage the issues in such instances is equally crucial in terms of the kind of process that will be structured. Since we cannot always avoid the negation of ourselves, the violation of the process, or even our own vulnerability to collusion with these violations (Levenson, 1972, 1983; Sandler, 1976), the critical issue is how to turn such occurrences into analytic opportunities (Fromm-Reichmann, 1950).

In this regard, my view is that, paradoxically, the analyst's greatest strength in such contexts may come not from the assertion of authority, such as by telling the patient what he or she must do, but from an acknowledgment of the analyst's own vulnerability and limits and of his or her *un*willingness to participate in a destructive relationship or to be used in nonanalytic ways. The analyst must insist that each participant has choices and is responsible for his or her behavior in relation to the other and in relation to the analytic endeavor. One cannot use the limitations and failings of the other, or the fact of provocation by the other, to exempt oneself from responsibility for one's own behavior. The emphasis is on process and relationship, on recognition of agency, and on the necessity for a collaborative engagement. In effect, this kind of engagement can in itself become an important kind of new experience.

The premise is that there is a difference between facilitating an opportunity to deal with destructive emotions or impulses in an analytic way, which can be a healing and integrative experience, and allowing for these to be acted out, which can be undermining and reinforce the patient's cynicism and despair, and which can create iatrogenic problems. The analyst's way of participating plays a vital role in shaping which of these kinds of transference-countertransference developments will occur.

Some additional clinical examples follow.

MARILYN

Marilyn, a single woman in her thirties, began a session by telling me she was angry at me because I had left an opened letter lying on my desk and she had been unable to resist reading it. She stated that if a child has a problem stealing and the mother leaves money lying around then the mother is guilty of complicity.

I noted that her reaction seemed similar to her reaction in the prior session when she had inquired about the occasion for flowers in my office that day. She had become angry when I would not give the details and had stated self-righteously that if I were not prepared to answer her question I had no business having the flowers.

Her response was so provocative that I had to resist my own impulse to respond in a hostile way. After some thought I remarked that there were two issues. One had to do with her feelings, and the other had to do with her behavior and its impact. I stated that, although I felt responsive to her obvious pain, her accusations and blame were very provocative. I also added that, although it was clear that it was difficult for her to take "no" for an answer or to deal with her disappointment and hurt, she had to respect my right to say "no." Interestingly, having said this, I no longer felt angry but rather curious.

She began to cry and said she felt she couldn't do anything right. My comments had made her feel worthless and hopeless. She stated that all she wanted was my love and approval, but she did not know how to get it.

I focused on the extent of her pain when she was disappointed, on the extent to which she became coercive in response to frustration, and on its impact on others.

She softened as we talked about this and offered associations to an interaction with a man she had dated over the weekend. During the date he told her about another woman with whom he was involved. She reported that she found this so painful that she had to leave. This was obviously relevant to her reactions to the flowers and the letter, both of which were indicative of my connections with others.

This was followed by an association to how excluded she felt from her parents' relationship as a child. She cried as she elaborated that she couldn't even bear to admit how much it mattered to her then, that she felt the same feelings now toward me, as well as in relation to the man. She described fights with her father in which he wouldn't talk to her for days if she didn't do things his way, and instances where the only way she could get what she wanted from her parents was by bullying them and making them feel guilty as she had tried to do with me. She stated that I was the first person who had stood up to her when she bullied, instead of succumbing, rejecting her altogether, or remaining uninvolved.

What we were now able to see was that she had assumed it was her "love" that turned other people away. Her view was that it was "poisonous," "voracious," "demanding," "coercive." I pointed out that it was not the love that was "poisonous" but her behavior when she felt frustrated. The problem was complicated by her reacting with rage to the idea that if she cared about another she was dependent, vulnerable, and at that person's mercy. She could not tolerate the fact that she could not control the other's responses when she would have liked to. She responded by saying that at times this felt like a life and death issue for her.

In the following sessions, she reported with some embarrassment how much this interaction with me had meant to her. Then, in a subsequent session she described an incident with a man she had begun to date. Rather than try to control and manipulate him, she was able to tell him how vulnerable she felt as she began to become more seriously interested in him. He told her that the thing he liked about her was her honesty and lack of pushiness. She began to cry because it was the first time in her life that she felt she had been that way. She felt "great" she said, and elaborated that she now realized she could be "soft" without being a "wimp." She described feeling excited and proud, feeling for the first time like an adult, and feeling good about herself whether or not the relationship worked out. She stated that it was a breakthrough for her that she could be this open. She no longer feared that she would not be able to tolerate or survive frustration, and she did not need to become "ugly" and "controlling." She had a new sense of dignity and self-respect.

Many months later, when Marilyn had begun to live with the man with whom she had become involved at the time just reported, she related the following dream:

"I was awakened by a phone call. A friend wanted to make plans. I was aware it would take me away from lying in bed with my boyfriend. While I am lying in bed I am aware that around my

vagina are beautiful purple violets with black seeds. The doorbell rings and I have to get out of bed to answer it and make arrangements with the person at the door. I had a sense of not wanting to lose any of the seeds. I try to catch them as I get up but I don't catch all of them."

Her associations were:

"I think it has to do with having babies. I don't want to lose the seeds. I feel like I have to hold onto them for a while though, because it's not quite time yet. I think the violets are related to our last session and to my feelings about myself as a woman. I feel a potential for flowering and feeling pleased rather than feeling I am damaged or missing something or inadequate. It's interesting that violets are my mother's favorite flowers. It's interesting that I would choose that flower."

There were associations to her mother and to her sense that her mother suffered from the same sense of dependency on a man to define her worth and identity with which she was struggling.

I present this dream because violets were the predominant flower in the bouquet in my office that had been the center of the earlier interaction. Although in the dream there was a sense of things still to work out, she had, nevertheless, achieved her own "violets."

In the following example I focus on the degree to which use of encounter, however effective, itself has transference-countertransference meanings, and constitutes a level of potential enactment that must also be acknowledged and addressed.

JANE

Jane often acted in hostile ways toward me without taking responsibility for her behavior, which included giving me checks that would inevitably bounce and then being very apologetic about her "oversight." She seemed so genuinely concerned that initially I found myself seduced into accepting her apology and assuming it would not happen again. But as these incidents recurred I commented to her that I realized it was not just an "oversight." I indicated that I now thought it was important to try to understand the seemingly hostile element of her behavior and its meaning. Simply to accept the apology and to go on from there would be to let her off the hook.

Although I expected protestations to the contrary, she was surprisingly receptive to my suggestion. In fact, she began to describe how "bad" she thought she was and even conceded that when she acts in hostile ways she gets so manifestly upset and proffers such good explanations and apologies that others do not get angry at her.

I made the point that it might be relevant to explore what she considered her "badness," since this was a recurring concern. My own association, which I shared, was to some material she had reported earlier in our work, in which she had expressed the same sense of her own intrinsic "badness." At that time she had described an incident when she was about five or six years old, during which she and some other older children had tied up a retarded girl and then took turns sticking needles into her belly. My remembering this previous incident shocked her for several reasons. First, she had not thought about this incident for a very long time. Second, she hadn't remembered that she had told me about it. Third, she was surprised that I remembered it at all.

In this context, as we began to consider whether her sense of "badness" had to do with some sense of her own potential sadism, she began to sob as I had never heard her sob before. She cried for the rest of the session in loud wailing tones, literally shaking from head to toe.

During the following session she stated that, though she thought my confronting her with all this was sadistic on my part, and she resented it, this was the first time she had ever really faced her own "sadism." She was surprised how relieved she felt in response. She then spoke about her own sense of how deceptive and devious she could be, always acting "nice" and "innocuous," but recognizing how inauthentic she was. She felt that for the first time she had been "discovered" and "understood."

Associations followed to her mother and to how her mother also had always been so "nice." Paradoxically, as a result they had remained isolated and cut off from one another. She now wondered whether each had treated the other as well as herself as too "fragile."

This was followed by further associations to another incident in her childhood, similar to the one with the retarded girl. She mentioned that both incidents had occurred when her mother had been pregnant and spoke about her ambivalent feelings about the pregnancy. She was then able to consider the obvious implications this had with regard to sticking needles into the girl's belly and to describe her fear at the time that the girl might have died as a result of what had been done to her. Then she thought, she would be found out and put in jail, and her own mother, whom she had never told about this incident, would find out what she had done. She also described realizing that her guilt was compounded by the fact she had had murderous feelings toward her own sister at that time and felt these were also being enacted with the retarded girl. Further, she talked about how traumatic it had been when her new sibling later was born retarded; she had assumed it had been her responsibility.

Given that Jane's wish, as described in Chapter 5, was to have others "care enough" to "rattle" her "gates" and "to come find her out," especially when she made it difficult, and especially when she did seem to be "fragile," and that this in fact was a sexual turn-on when it occurred, the meaning of my "finding her out" in this instance may be more complex than first appears. I raise this only to emphasize that as we deal with any issue, however productively, we are always involved in subtle kinds of enactment on other levels. Being alert to this allows us to expand the analytic exploration in potentially powerful ways.

JUSTIN

Justin had a history of getting into power struggles with therapists and his therapy relationships inevitably ended as these escalated out of control. Several years into our work a situation arose in which he fell one or two months behind in his payments and failed to catch up. (See Chapter 5 for details of the beginning phase of our work.)

Although I tried to explore this, he insisted it was simply a matter of economics, out of his control, and refused to discuss it further. I noted that I felt it was not so simple, but that I did not think it was worth getting into a power struggle over. (I had no reason based on experience to doubt that he would pay me.) He seemed a little surprised that I was not making the late payments more of an issue. He then acknowledged his appreciation of my patience and noted that he felt "special" because of it. Yet, he also reported that he was worried he was somehow manipulating me. (I wondered whether instead the issue was that he was failing to manipulate me into the kind of power struggle he seemed to want or that he might be concerned that I was somehow manipulating him. Certainly the scenario was not evolving as he had anticipated.)

Associations followed to his relationships with women, both those overtly sexual and those only covertly so. He noted, elaborating on material he had discussed before, that he was aware that he tended to structure these in terms of eroticized power struggles. He would set up "fidelity," for example, as the woman's requirement, and then feel oppressed by it and become angry at the woman in a way that was erotically charged. Then he would inevitably rebel against this "oppression" by being unfaithful, ostensibly to preserve his "autonomy and freedom." The whole scenario was a "turn-on." He then marveled at the fact that he did not seem to harbor angry feelings towards me, and he seemed confused and even frustrated. In fact, he expressed a longing to be able to get into a fight with me.

The question of whether he was trying to structure this kind of interaction between us was now raised, as he expressed some curiosity as to how I was able to avoid getting into a power struggle with him, since that was the way all of his prior therapeutic relationships had ended up.

Then, in a session sometime later, he came in and paid his total bill, announcing how good he felt about being able to do this now. It was clear that paying at this point was no less complex than not paying had been earlier. When I asked him how he understood this, he hypothesized that owing me money had been a way of keeping a connection going. In his mind it meant he could not walk out on me. Once he was paid up he was free to leave at any time. I wondered out loud if his owing me money also meant I couldn't "walk out on him," but he rejected this idea. Instead he indicated that he believed paying me now reflected his wish for our relationship to become "clean." He then proceeded to virtually contradict all of this, as he revealed a complex sexual fantasy that paying the bill was an act of compliance and submission, which for him generally involved erotic pleasure. He elaborated that this gave him a sense of being the woman's "sexual slave" and that he found himself both excited and angry about being in this position. He noted that he felt "turned on" by the concept and by the anger itself.

He elaborated further that there was also a manipulative aspect to this. He imagined that through his compliance he would get my approval, win me over, and then he would be able to "coast and get away with things." (I wondered why now and not before, but I did not interrupt his flow and let him continue.) He described a "shock of recognition" that these kinds of fantasies were characteristic of his relationships with women in general, and an awareness of how this obviously was now an integral part of his relationship to me.

He then described how he saw me as a "hot tamale" because I didn't let anything slide by. His view was that by not getting into the power struggle with him I was "forcing" him to face what he otherwise would avoid, thereby making him "submit," the very thing that turned him on.

There were detailed associations to past relationships with his mother and sister, and with girlfriends.

He then reported that in this very process he had been "forced" to stay in touch with his own experience more than he had ever been able to before. He was surprised to discover that he could. In this context he described feeling a new sense of curiosity about the nature of "internal experience" and about the analytic process.

Although I have argued for the value and importance of encounter, I think these examples help to emphasize the complexity of what is generated by this kind of analyst participation. There are always transference-countertransference meanings to what is thereby enacted which have to be closely monitored, and every interaction, however productive, opens new questions on a different level.

With those patients who seem to use the analytic relationship as an arena for destructive acting out, unless the destructiveness is engaged, the "work" may simply become a dangerous form of collusion, which can have serious negative iatrogenic consequences. What is crucial in such instances, to achieve a viable analytic process, *is that the analyst be able to understand the patient's vulnera-*

bility and the patient's ways of destroying or being destructive, and be sensitive to both the vulnerability and the destructiveness without being intimidated by either. In some such instances this means clarifying the ways the patient murders psychic possibilities, internal as well as external, and the contempt and despair implicit in varying forms of "spacing out" and going through motions. Nothing less than the patient's psychic aliveness and integrity may be at stake. At times it may even be a question of literal aliveness.

For example, a ten-year-old child, with acute life-threatening asthma, dreamt: *"There was some form of imposter that was me. My parents saw the imposter and thought it was me. I lost my chance to tell them it was an imposter."*

My work with him consisted of "finding him" and enabling him to hold onto himself at moments when he could no longer quite distinguish himself from the imposter he could pretend to be. As he was confronted with the ways in which he negated his own perceptions, thoughts and feelings in our immediate interaction, he began to experience much anxiety, and for the first time to experience aggressive fantasies. In this context he literally began to breathe more deeply. In fact, the asthma, which had required many visits to hospital emergency rooms in the middle of the night, began to abate dramatically.

Clearly there are times when "analyses" can serve as holding operations and can become interminable, without any real growth occurring (Winnicott, 1969). Khan (1969) describing a phenomenon he calls "symbiotic omnipotence," writes that at times the patient's ability to function, sometimes extraordinarily well, by virtue of maintaining a specific kind of relation to the analyst, may not be a positive development at all. It may reflect an analytic stalemate based on a form of collusion.

Some might argue that at times such use of the analyst may in fact allow for an experience of creative discovery and can become the basis of growth, so that it may be appropriate not to intervene too quickly (see Searles on the positive value of therapeutic symbiosis, 1979). It may be, for example, that using the analyst this way serves to allay Promethean fears of being independent, creative, or functioning on one's own, and allows the patient to engage in an important kind of imaginative exploration that would not be possible otherwise. The counter-argument is that an analytic resolution would require that the Promethean fears be engaged. If this does not occur the patient remains in many ways as limited by them as before. The challenge here may rest with the issue of timing and balance.

Some patients are so concerned about being "good" patients that they try to push themselves to go "forward" with the work despite their own internal resistance. Ironically, this can constitute an even more formidable form of resistance. It might be conceived of as resistance to engaging the internal resistance by attempting to bypass it altogether; it becomes, in effect, a way of precluding rather than engaging in an analytic process. This has some similarity to what has been traditionally referred to as "flight into health" or a form of manic defense (see Winnicott, 1935). Alternatively, it may reflect the enactment of some complex fantasy about submitting to the analyst, or it may be a way of protecting against fears of varying forms of internal threat. This is the dilemma we face in the common situation where a patient makes a decision to explore certain feelings counterphobically or out of compliance. Though such an exploration might be productive it may also be problematic.

One patient, for example, had a history of getting into very dangerous and demeaning sexual involvements by virtue of a counterphobic pattern of deciding to "give herself," often quite masochistically. My view was that to let her proceed this way in the analytic context, even though the dangers were obviously not comparable, and even though it seemed overtly to be the analytically motivated way, might be tantamount to playing into her masochistic way of submitting herself. In this instance my effort to clarify whether a form of masochistic submission was being enacted, rather than to allow it to be replayed once again, met with her resistance.

She argued that I was not letting her proceed "analytically" and that I was cutting off an important analytic moment. Nevertheless, as I stressed my view that it was important to understand the basis for her decision to "tell all" despite her evident fears, she revealed that she had been worried that I was more interested in "scoring an analytic success" than in her feelings. It now seemed that she had been testing me, not necessarily consciously, by "offering herself," in this case "analytically."

If I simply had let her proceed, this might never have been revealed.

Encounter involves more than identifying the critical issues. It involves a very personal engagement, as analyst and patient come up against each other and have to take responsibility for themselves in relation to each other. The fact that what goes on interactively can be talked about explicitly creates a unique kind of intimacy that adds even more dimensions to the experience. This kind of engagement not only helps expand awareness but also provides a medium for working through, as the negotiation of how to relate in a way that will be acceptable to both and analytically viable becomes the locus of therapeutic action, as well as its medium.

CHAPTER 10

Abuse and Desire

WORKING WITH MALE AND female patients who have been heterosexually or homosexually abused during childhood, especially by a parent, I have observed that these experiences have very specific effects on the individual's subsequent patterns of relation to desire, not just of a sexual nature, but in a much more pervasive sense. This, in turn, has specific impact on patterns of and capacity for relationship. Here I will present some of my observations and hypotheses about the relationship between sexual abuse and desire, and about specific questions of technique as they arise in analysis.

Though sexual abuse by *anyone* is a horrendous violation, when it is by one's parent — the very person one is dependent on for care and protection — it is even more devastating. Beyond the trauma of the violation of one's body, the child also has to deal with the experience of betrayal by the parent, and usually also by the other parent for having failed to protect the child, with or without awareness. This can be so overwhelming that it leads to a virtual collapse of the child's psychic world. In some cases the child may engage in extremely complex and often debilitating forms of denial and dissociation in a desperate effort to try to hold his or her internal world together, which ironically results in splitting and disintegration of another sort.

Where the child was brutalized and there was no way to resist, the sense of helplessness, pain, panic, and rage is often so extreme and unbearable that the experience simply cannot be contained. This is particularly so if the victim was sexually aroused by the sensual and physical contact, sometimes to his or her own surprise and/or horror. In such instances, in addition to the trauma of the betrayal by the parent, the child may experience a sense of betrayal by his or her own body.

Where the sexual involvement with the parent was experienced as a fulfillment of the child's own fantasies, longings, and desires, it is problematic in another way. The child may feel the full responsibility lies with himself or herself. To the degree that arousal of the victim's own desire is experienced as the basis for the vulnerability, the relation to desire becomes especially troublesome. This is particularly so when the relationships in question endured a long time, perhaps years, and when it was clear that unless the child had been a cooperative participant and derived some gratification from the involvement the relationship could not have been possible.

Often there is some confusion as to who stimulated whom and who is responding to whom and why. Ferenczi (1933) suggests that the child's experience of desire may reflect a form of compliance or collusion with what the child unconsciously understands to be the parent's needs and desires, which then become experienced as his or her own. To the degree that this is true it may reflect a convoluted act of compassion on the part of the child towards the parent. The complex internal gymnastics serve to absolve the parent of responsibility and to deny the child's experience of helplessness and betrayal. It may be easier for the child to engage in a subtle form of identification with the aggressor than to face the betrayal by the parent and both the sense of internal devastation and the overwhelming emotions he or she would be subject to otherwise. The child may even suffer a sense of guilt for not being able to cure the parent of his or her problem, in addition to the guilt about his or her own participation in whatever form it may have taken. Where this is the case, the child may be left with terrifying feelings of helplessness and vulnerability, as well as equally terrifying and contradictory feelings of guilt and omnipotence.

The cumulative impact of sexual abuse, given any of these internal scenarios and any of the multitude of other possible internal scenarios that may evolve, is often so overwhelming that many aspects of internal and external reality are dissociated or denied. In some instances this may result in "out of body" experiences. Even the identification with the aggressor seems to be a variant on this, serving as a means to escape from internal experiences that are unbearable, to get "outside" of oneself when being "inside" is intolerable. Experiences of disorganization, decompensation, and disintegration are also common.

The devastating states of extreme confusion, or even madness, which these forms of psychic violence then create can have crippling effects on the child's continuing development, and in turn on the child's already diminished sense of self-esteem, serving to intensify feelings of helplessness, humiliation, shame, and self-contempt. This constitutes yet another kind of trauma, now in the form of a betrayal by the victim's own psyche.

Where massive dissociation and denial occur, patients often come for treatment with no memories of having been abused, so that it is only late in treatment that this comes to light. Or, if they do remember it is without any feeling. The initial presenting complaints often focus on terrifying experiences of derealization and depersonalization involving somatic symptoms and anxiety attacks, varying kinds of "out of body" experiences, generalized cognitive and perceptual impairments, difficulty maintaining a sense of a cohesive self, difficulties relating to others including fears of "knowing" and of being "known," and difficulties with regard to taking "action" in varying ways.

A dramatic example of how extreme the latter can become was evidenced by one patient who was unable to ring the office doorbell during the early phases of our work. She felt it was too "intrusive." If I did not look outside the door of my waiting room at the appointed hour and ask her to come in, she would simply stand there indefinitely. For her the "action" of ringing the doorbell was a highly charged and symbolically complex act.

All the victims of abuse I have worked with have been involved in varying kinds of sadomasochistic enactments in their lives, particularly in their sexual lives, whether overt or covert. They also reported various compulsive and addictive behaviors, including compulsive use of alcohol and drugs, which became more or less prominent during different periods of their lives.[12]

In all cases, helping these patients to grasp the fact that the burden of guilt and responsibility for the abusive relationship lies with the abusing adult, no matter what the child's role may have been, is crucial. This is especially important in those instances in which the child may have derived some sort of gratification from the involvement and after the first contact actively sought the physical relationship. Clarifying the ways and the degree to which their desire and vulnerability were exploited by the abusing adults — no matter what the child's role may have been — becomes a pivotal issue in treatment and has profound ramifications with regard to the individual's ultimate relation to his or her own desire.

For some victims of abuse, coming to terms with their own participation in these early relationships requires recognizing that they participated at all. This allows for reclaiming disavowed aspects of self and aids in the resolution of varying forms of alienation from and/or repudiation of desire resulting from dissociation and denial. It also allows for clarification of the limits of the victim's power and responsibility in interpersonal relationships. In some such instances this has proved to be the key to the resolution of dynamically motivated confusion of fantasy and reality, as the patient finally was able to relate to and confront his or her own need to maintain such confusion.

One patient was able to realize that because she knew some of her views of the abusive experience involved fabrications that were elaborations of what actually had occurred, it had become reasonable for her to conclude that she could not trust any of her perceptions as to what was fact and what was fantasy. She thus described a state, reported by other patients as well, of feeling, *"Maybe I made it all up. Maybe I dreamed it. Maybe it never really happened. Maybe it was a figment of my imagination."*

It seemed that it was easier for her to "space out" and become confused about her own perceptions and experience than it was to deal with the pain of her feelings about what had occurred and about her own responsiveness. She described becoming fascinated with the idea that she could *"leave my body . . . take my mind somewhere else . . . like time travel in my head."*

This patient, who had been abused by an uncle, expressed her fear that if she really had acknowledged what was happening she might have had to tell someone about it. Her fantasy was that her father, upon finding out, would have killed her uncle; then he would have been tried for murder and gone to jail, and she would have been responsible for the destruction of the whole fabric of the family's life.

She developed a pattern of knowing something was happening but acting as though nothing was happening while it was going on. This pattern of "spacing out" or "numbing out," never knowing for sure what was real and what was fantasy, which left her somewhat helpless and paralyzed, became a characteristic way of dealing with experiences of all kinds, not just sexual experience.

A moment with another patient, which was dramatic because of its simplicity, helped reveal the extent of her wish not to have to see the ways in which she perpetuated the intertwining of reality and fantasy. It involved her remembering a dream and then refusing to tell me for fear of finding out my reaction. She stated that she believed she would not be able to deal with her disappointment if I did not respond in the hoped-for way. It was easier to avoid this kind of confrontation with reality and with having to engage her own experience.

Her conflicts, however, were not just about knowing. They also extended to her fears of being known. She described feeling, *"My power is in not letting anyone know me. They can't have it. It's mine."*

By asserting this "power" she believed she could live a double life, a kind of charade, in which she could participate overtly but actually drop out. In her view her body "stayed" but she "went" somewhere else. She became what she described as *"a secret hoarder of who I am."* Her fear was that intimacy with another human being, including the analyst, could threaten her very sense of intactness.

Intimacy was problematic in other ways as well. This patient, who would cringe in terror at moments of feeling close in the analytic interaction, also noted a link to her eroticized fantasy about a relationship in which she gave herself completely, to the point of allowing herself to be violated, humiliated, degraded, dehumanized.

"I feel so repulsed I almost feel nauseated. . . . Why should I feel excitement about being abused and humiliated? It's one thing to admit you have been abused. It's another thing to say there is a part of you that finds it sexually exciting. I guess this feels like a huge dark secretive part of myself."

For this patient, who had never named or verbalized the abusive experience before, this verbalizing called up intense feelings about the sexual experiences that had not been previously accessible, and about her own internal situation now.

Explication of the full extent of the patient's *presumption* of guilt about having provoked or enjoyed the abuse by virtue of his or her own desire or fantasy, and often also about not having been able to cure the parent so that the parent would not have acted abusively, can be pivotal. Working this through so that the victim begins to really understand that the responsibility and guilt belong to the adult, and that the situation was beyond the child's power and control, no matter what the child may have wished, generally leads to a dramatic abatement of the such symptoms as derealization and depersonalization experiences, somatic symptoms, anxiety attacks, and various "out of body" experiences. It also seems to allow for overcoming cognitive and perceptual impairments, for resolution of fears of "knowing" and of being "known," and for resolution of difficulties with regard to taking "action" in varying ways.

The dilemma is how to establish a relationship where this can be achieved with someone who, after having been betrayed by a parent, understandably is not likely to be open to taking a risk on any kind of meaningful relationship. This is even more problematic in those cases where the patient may not even be aware of having been abused. Furthermore, because the mental state of such patients is generally quite fragile, any effort on the part of the analyst to engage the patient may be experienced as a form of violation or intrusion threatening the tenuous integration that has been established. The need to be sensitive to the significance of everything that occurs interactively is paramount with these patients, for whom relationships are so readily structured and/or experienced in terms of intrusion, co-option, violation, or seduction; where the roles of victim and abuser often shift back and forth; and where there may be a real risk of decompensation and breakdown.

The challenge is how to create a context of adequate safety so that very painful and threatening material can be worked through in a constructive way. If these patients can be helped to deal with the feared material without being overwhelmed to the point of decompensating, this can be the most healing and strengthening experience of all. In contrast, if the emotions become overwhelming and there is a breakdown or loss of control, or the patient becomes homicidal or suicidal, this can be devastating, as his or her worst fears are confirmed.

In a sense the analyst's protection of the patient from the threat of such decompensation, as he or she slows the process down so that the patient does not become overwhelmed, and as he or she is careful not to intrude or co-opt the patient in any way, such as by interpreting or even asking questions (which at times may be experienced by such patients as a form of rape), is a definition of what it means to provide a "context of safety." The important issue here from my perspective is not the defensive denial or dissociation; rather, it is the *vulnerability* that is the basis for the need for defense in the first place.

Facilitating an opportunity for the patient to discover that it is possible to talk about devastating experiences without decompensating in the present is not easy. Any verbalization on the part of the analyst may be experienced as some form of intrusion or violation, and any failure to respond may be experienced as rejection and neglect. Moreover, the pulls toward inadvertently engaging in sadomasochistic kinds of enactment can be subtle and powerful. In this regard, simply encouraging these patients — for whom revealing themselves or not revealing themselves, knowing and being known, have such complex symbolic meaning — to formulate or explore their own experience can become such an enactment.

Any effort to address what is going on explicitly between analyst and patient, or to explicate the interactive subtleties, can also be a form of pressure for patients whose mode of coping has been to not let themselves fully acknowledge what they were experiencing, especially as they were experiencing it. Therefore, the analyst has to make himself or herself available without imposing his or her views or needs for acknowledgment, explication, or movement.

A countertransference dilemma that presents itself in such contexts is how to walk the fine line between being respectful and careful not to intrude, on the one side, and being neglectful, on the other. What we must establish is a new experience in which the patient has the opportunity to realize that it is possible to be in a relationship without having to be pressured by another or required to submit to the other to sustain the relationship. How do we help the patient begin to recognize available but unseen choices when it is often hard to know whether our own behavior is analytically motivated or reflects a subtle form of countertransference enactment?

Another common countertransference dilemma with such patients is that the analyst may sometimes feel paralyzed, "spaced out," foggy, almost in a trancelike state, as though he or she has been deadened in some way; then he or she is unable to resist, or to even struggle to do so, and is not even aware of being in such a state at the time, much the way many of these patients feel much of the time.

Finally, given understandable countertransference fears of "blaming the victim," how can we help patients who have been victims of abuse to become sensitive not only to the real tragedy they have suffered at the hands of others, but also to the continuing one that they have become agents of themselves? Helping these patients to grasp how they murder psychic possibilities and foreclose the possibility of meaningful relationship and how violent this process is to internal as well as external life, is essential. The reclaiming of dissociated aspects of self becomes the key to the patient's becoming able to engage in a necessary process of mourning.

Here are some details from my work with two victims of childhood sexual abuse.

JUNE

June, an attractive professional women in her thirties who had had prior treatment with several therapists, entered treatment with me because of intense and frequent anxiety states, during which she experienced many psychosomatic symptoms. She began on a twice-a-week basis, eventually increasing to three times a week, as I will describe later. Her story unfolded as follows:

She was involved in a long-term sexual relationship with her father which she thought may have begun at about age eight and lasted until about age fourteen or fifteen.[13] The incestuous behavior consisted of his sucking her breasts and fingering her vaginal area. As the years went on, these incidents began to occur only while he was under the influence of alcohol. There was no actual intercourse. She pretended always to be asleep.

In the course of our work together she came for the first time to recognize that *"I wanted it then as much as my father did."* She went on: *"Although I thought all these years my disgust was for my father, I now realize my disgust is for my own participation and the pleasure I got out of something I accepted as wrong."*

She described her realization of her own active participation as an "epiphanous understanding" that unlocked enormous emotions and memories. She felt it also allowed her to recognize the impact the early experience with her father had had on all her relationships with men, and especially on her relation to her own sexuality. She related her general pattern of "not being there" and feeling no pleasure in or desire for sex in her adult years to these early sexual experiences.

As she now saw it, the relationship with her father not only was sexual but also served as a kind of compensation for what she described as the "emotional poverty" of her life at home.

"I experienced the sexual attention as finally one of my parents was giving me some emotional attention. It made me feel favorite, special, loved."

With father who often lost control and became violent physically in their day-to-day relationship, the sexual moments were surprisingly tender.[14]

She also noted that her awareness of her appeal to him gave her a sense of power and control in relation to him that she had experienced in no other way.

An important insight was that *"My father stepped into a role at the age when I was looking for a player anyway."* She further realized that *"In assuming the role of my lover he abandoned for me his role as a father."*

Nevertheless, there remained a degree of confusion as to the extent of both her power and her helplessness. She was never sure to what degree either was responding to cues from the other or from each one's own desire.

Eventually she was able to articulate a recognition that her mother was an equally important figure in this drama. She described how her own shutting out of her mother, which her mother did not protest, was integral to her involvement with her father and in some ways set the stage for it.

In this sense she came to feel that she had been abandoned and betrayed by both parents in terms of their parental responsibility. Yet there was also some question in her own mind as to her motives for not turning to her mother at the time.

She indicated that at the time her conscious fear had been that, if she were to have told her mother, her mother would have had a violent reaction and might have left her father, breaking up the family. She also had imagined that if she were to have told anyone else it would have gotten back to her parents with even worse repercussions. The question of whom she was protecting was obviously very complex. At a later time she spoke of her terror then that to try to end the abuse would have caused a blowup of such proportions that all that would have been left would have been a "violent void"—there would have been nothing else.

Another aspect of her dilemma involved the length of the abuse: the longer she did not protest and speak up the harder it was to do so, because each time she let it go on she only *"got in deeper."* Yet, as she also emphasized in treatment, she had never actually "named" what was happening, even to herself. She never called it anything, never described it to herself *"out loud in my mind,"* and certainly never talked about it with him. She developed what she called *"an ability not to look at what I didn't want to look at."*

This pattern of knowing something was happening but acting as though nothing was happening while it was going on and/or resisting facing what was going on persisted throughout June's adult life and became a characteristic way of dealing with experiences of all kinds, not just sexual ones.

Over time, June came to realize that the situation of being aroused and then not satisfied left her not only with guilt and but also with frustration. In her view she thus suffered a *"double whammy,"* a kind of *"double jeopardy."*

She also noted that the relationship with her father ended when she decided to no longer pretend to be asleep. If he was aware she was awake when he entered the room her father would quickly leave.

June, as well as other female patients, described eventually reaching a point of not being able to experience sexual pleasure, of being turned off, shut down. The cutting off of desire extended beyond sexual desire to wishes and feelings in general, even to intellectual curiosity and development. Apparently not to desire or to experience desire or pleasure sexually became a way for these women to free themselves from feelings of guilt and fear about their desires and their power, as well as the lurking concern that father's behavior was in response to their own fantasies or desires or their own seductive behavior. It also protected them from being vulnerable to the advances of another and from the sexual fantasies that were so exciting and yet so disturbing.

The detachment and lack of feeling that thus evolved continued into adult life and ended up having a paradoxical effect. Instead of serving as the protection it seemed designed to be, it actually allowed them to tolerate levels of abuse and violence that otherwise might have been unbearable. June described one relationship in which she was often physically threatened by her boyfriend, once with an iron. Other patients also reported very self-destructive patterns of relation.

Eventually the "deadness" that resulted from the cutting off became oppressive in its own right. Some patients began to use drugs.

As June found she could be more responsive while she was under the influence of alcohol, she began to rely on the use of alcohol more and more. Nevertheless, she reached a point when the feelings of detachment became so frightening for her that even the alcohol did not help. There were descriptions of *"spacing out"* to such a degree that it was not possible to *"find the way back."*

In such instances the feelings of derealization and depersonalization became terrifying. These often involved feelings of nonexistence, of not being in her body, of no sense of any boundary or membrane around her body, of a *"horrible diffuse state."*

June described images of *"dissolving into particles"* and of a sense of losing herself and being unable to stay intact inside her skin. There were feelings of floating in space, of being untethered, unmoored. She said it was like the opposite of an image of a fetus tied by an umbilical cord. It involved being totally unanchored, flowing into *"a bigger thing . . . with my edges going."*

There were experiences of palpitations, fears that she was dying of a heart attack, and frequent visits to hospital emergency rooms in the throes of these states.

By focusing on our interaction we were able to capture June's pattern of "turning off" her own emotions as it occurred. In a particular series of sessions June began to refer to me by name while talking to me. In the course of one session she might use my name repeatedly. Each time this happened I felt jarred in a way that was so subtle I almost let it slip by. My sense on reflection, however, was that this seemed to be, on the one hand, a kind of intimate expression, almost the way someone might use someone else's name in a moment of passion, and yet on the other, a way of putting the brakes on the evolving intimacy, a kind of "coming up for air" when it began to feel too intense.

I asked if she had any ideas about why she was using my name in this way now. What kind of emotion was she feeling as she was talking to me? Did it feel problematic or frightening to her in some way? (I wondered but did not ask, Were there any sexual feelings involved?)

I did ask explicitly whether she thought there might be some connection between her feelings now and her feelings during those sexual encounters with her father that she had related. Specifically, I had in mind her description of her inability to control herself in terms of giving in to the feelings of physical pleasure with her father despite her sense that it was wrong and she should resist. Was there a feeling of need now to control the flow of emotion out of some sense of fear?

June's reaction to my questioning the meaning of her use of my name was that she wanted to call me for an extra session immediately after leaving the office, but did not. What followed was a series of sessions of great intensity, involving vivid memories of details of sexual experiences that had not been accessible to her before, and a very emotional experience of great insight as to her own actual participation in these sexual scenes. This was actually the point at which she experienced her so-called "epiphanous insight" that she had wanted the incest as much as her father had. The result of all this was that she asked to increase her sessions from two to three times per week.

Eventually she was able to articulate her experience as follows:

"I realized I was a player rather than someone played on, and a player who had all the cards. But the sad thing is that I had no understanding, nor should I have been allowed to play this game. . . . I have an image of myself marching through with the world falling down. I think now the fact was I was doing some of the pulling down without even understanding this was the case."

What also became clear to her somewhat later was that her fear of the developing intimacy in the analytic relationship was based on a *"deeply laid belief that the nature of closeness is one of threat and exploitation."*

In the context of articulating all this June began to reclaim her own capacity to experience desire. The new insights also enabled her to penetrate the defensive need to keep herself in a state of confusion and detachment.

As June became increasingly able to realize, through the actual analytic interaction, that there were behaviors and responses on the part of others, including both analyst and father, for which she could not be held responsible, even if they were congruent with her own fantasies, there was a dramatic diminution of the anxiety symptoms, and she was able to give up using alcohol.

There were now intense experiences of anger, grief, tears. What emerged also was a new sense of compassion about her own participation in the incestuous relationship and about the pathos, pathology, and limitations of her father and mother, both of whom had been victims of abuse themselves.

She now described a new sense of clarity about the degree to which she had been in a constant state of overstimulation during the incest period without realizing it. She speculated that her sexual acting out and multiple pregnancies during her adolescence may have been a way of unconsciously discharging the sexual tension that had been generated in her physical relationship with her father, and that even as these pregnancies were a kind of rebellion against her father, as well as a way of creating a scandal in her middle-class community, on another level they were a symbolic fulfillment of her relationship with him. Her view was that the babies were probably his babies in her mind.

She also realized that she had somehow always felt the "real" her was the one who had participated in the sex and the rest was just a facade. She began to see her own responsiveness as natural. As she put it, *"What else would a child do?"*

(Another patient had a similar realization regarding her compulsive masturbation as a child: *"Though I thought then I was depraved and a pervert, I now realize it was in response to overstimulation and I never had a chance."*)

June's anger now focused on her mother's failure to protect her not only from her father's transgressions but also from her own vulnerability.

Following the articulation of all of this June began to experience periods in which she felt intensely vulnerable in ways in which she had never allowed herself to feel before, both in and out of treatment. A sense of longing emerged for contact with women as well as with men. She now began to see her ability to be open and vulnerable as an indication of her strength and sensitivity and a basis for the possibility of intimacy. In a sense her former perceptions of reality were now turned inside out.

As with the other patients, as the anxiety symptoms diminished over the course of the work, and as June became much more "present" in her relationships, in treatment as well as elsewhere, an even more intensive kind of exploration became possible. Her own image was that whereas in the past she always felt she was functioning with a *"veil in place, like a curtain,"* she now had access to that part of herself, *"whatever that part is,"* that seemed to be behind the curtain.

Interestingly, at this point she expressed concern about being *"irreparably flawed,"* and an understanding that her fear of analysis had been precisely the fear of finding out that she could not "fix" herself, that she could not be cured. A further insight was that in the past she had always assumed that whatever was wrong was because of her own "flawedness." At this point she was clear in her own mind about the extent of the "flawedness" of her parents, of her need not to see it, of the fact that it was not "her fault" or her responsibility to cure it, and of its impact on her.

Over time she became increasingly able to recognize the ways in which her lack of responsiveness, in bed as well as in virtually every other situation, had to do with her own internal issues. She could tell when it was a response to specific qualities of the other and what was going on (or not going on) in her relationships. This included a growing — and important — realization of a tendency when things went wrong to attribute it to the fact of the abuse and to assume it was all her responsibility when this might not have been warranted. This became a block to really confronting what the other might be doing or not doing in the present that was problematic in its own terms.

With regard to the countertransference dilemma of how the analyst deals with his or her own feelings of paralysis, spacing out, and inability to stay engaged, as tends to occur with such patients, I would like to note that there were instances with June when this did occur for me. Though at times I felt too immobilized to do or say anything, there were other moments when, perhaps out of my own despair and perhaps because of a need to reassure myself of my own aliveness, I began to pick up on details of what she had brought just because they interested me, not necessarily because I thought they were analytically significant. This often led to very lively and enlivening discussions of movies, books, restaurants, recipes, plays, science, current events, poetry, philosophy, even psychoanalysis. These seemed, to my surprise, to be important in ways I could not have anticipated.

For example, she reported after these discussions an increasing sense of her own intellectual and critical capabilities. It thus seemed that it was not only the enlivening effect of these conversations, but also the opportunity they provided for her to experience her own intellectual capabilities, that seemed significant. She reported discovering intellectual and critical capabilities she was not aware of having and feeling that for the first time she could *"give credence to my own ideas."* The feelings this evoked were like a kind of "high" in which she had a sense that things she had not imagined before were "possible."

The opportunity for her to discover that it was possible to engage in a way where we both could really enjoy each other, and in which there was no pressure for either of us to submit to the other, seemed important as well.

Once we were thus extricated from the paralytic moment and were engaged in a lively and mutually present way, it became possible to begin to address what had gone on when we were both so "spaced out" or so "locked in."

All of these changes made possible yet another level of analytic exploration, in which issues in relation to her mother as well as to her father could be addressed in new ways. She began to consider the *triangular* nature of the incestuous situation and to struggle with her complex feelings about her relationship with her mother.

From this vantage point it appeared that my refusal to remain in a paralyzed deadened state or to be locked into the painful kind of interaction that had been evolving, as well as my ability to find my way out of it independently, turned out to be not simply a way of indulging my own need but also an extremely important analytic step. Once again, I was impressed with the degree to which new experience within the analytic relationship can become a locus of therapeutic action.

It may be of interest that a very powerful and moving subsequent phase of my work with June, some years later, involved a period of months during which we were each moved to tears, session after session, literally going though boxes of tissues, as she finally dealt with feelings about her pregnancy when she was eighteen years old and how it had been handled, and about the baby she had given up for adoption. This work culminated in a decision to try to find her child. There was much anxiety as she finally initiated a search, and much emotion anticipating both finding and not finding him. Her efforts ultimately were successful. This led to a period of much agonizing about whether to make herself known to him. There were many more shared moments of deep emotion and tears as the woman who had been so "numb," so unable to feel anything for so long, struggled not only with her feelings about having found her child, but also with her feelings about what it meant to reclaim herself.

CARL

Carl, an attractive man in his late twenties who described himself as homosexual, began treatment on a once-a-week basis expressing fears that I might try to convert him to heterosexuality. In the early months of our work I was clearly on trial, as he studied and evaluated me. I in turn focused on all the interactive nuances, as I tried to help him articulate his anxieties and recognize and deal with his complex feelings about choosing whether and how he wanted to use our relationship. I was clear that these were his choices, that I would respect his wishes, and that I did not want him to tell me anything more than he wanted to, even though I felt it would be important to talk about his feelings of not wanting to if this were the case.

It took six months before he trusted me enough to tell me that he was afraid that if he told me his fantasies I would be so disgusted I would not want to see him again. Interestingly, in this context he decided he did want to reveal them to me, to take that chance. He articulated them as follows:

His sexual fantasies involved dominating, raping, degrading, enslaving, dehumanizing and murdering other men. He reported images of having them stuffed and mounted as trophies. His fear was that he might lose control and act out his violent fantasies.

"You read in the papers about these guys who do these horrendous things, and all the neighbors say 'he was such a nice guy.' My fear is that I will snap some day and really go out and do something like that, that there really is a very crazy side to me."

He stated that he was afraid to even look at me as he told me all of this, and yet that he also felt a kind of relief. He also noted that he did not have a sense of himself as separate from his fantasies or any hope that these could change. Then, through tears, he added, *"A long time ago I gave up thinking there was any other choice. I accepted I was fucked up and I would have to live with it."*

In his daily behavior, including his relation to me, he described himself as timid, desperate for approval, afraid to say no. All of this felt humiliating. In contrast, in his fantasies he felt a sense of power.

He elaborated further that he had hair and leather fetishes that dated back to as young as five years old, and that he often went to

S and M bars, where he found partners with whom he acted out some of his fantasies. He noted that, because these sadomasochistic relationships were carried out by mutual agreement, they didn't have the same charge as forcing the other to do something against his will. He described a number of instances in which he had gotten into situations where he felt endangered. Although these had been extremely exciting, they had been so terrifying that he finally sought treatment.

He indicated that there had never been anyone he had been able to talk about this aspect of his life to before, even though he had been in treatment twice before, and that being able to tell me all of this meant a great deal. It was a big step for him.

In the period following these exchanges he reported that he had decided he no longer wanted to be involved in the kind of violent and dangerous relationships he had engaged in before and that he wanted to terminate the sadomasochistic homosexual live-in relationship in which he was then engaged. (Much later, when he read this chapter, he stated that once he had told me about this relationship and it was no longer a secret it did not hold the same charge for him as before.)

At the time, after months of struggle and much violence between himself and his partner, he finally extricated himself from this very destructive relationship. Then he avoided all sexual relations for about one year. During this period, still working once a week, he struggled to try to understand why his violent fantasies and impulses were so compelling and why he remained terrified about asserting himself with me as well as with others.

What emerged at this point was a suggestion that to a certain extent he was "stuck" because he had an investment in not changing. In this context serious questions emerged about the degree to which he held onto his "pathology" as evidence that his mother had failed him, and about the degree to which he viewed this as placing him in a position of "power" in relation to her. (His father was no longer alive.) Articulating this allowed him to realize that his wishes to continue to hurt her conflicted with his wishes to try to work out his problems.

During this period, in which I insisted that he was the only one who could decide what he wanted, almost to his own surprise he found himself drawn to a young woman, despite great anxiety about whether she could possibly be interested in someone like himself.

She was responsive to his very tentative efforts at developing a friendship with her, and over time he became increasingly open with her about his sexual history. She seemed so accepting that he then tried to initiate a romantic involvement, and she was responsive. As this relationship then progressed, though he struggled with the old sadomasochistic fantasies, he began to find himself heterosexually responsive, which he had not imagined was possible.

As this relationship continued to develop he then had a dream, which he reported as follows: *"My father was trying to sexually abuse me and had murdered someone."*

At the time he noted that he felt this was an important dream, but he could not do much with it. Nevertheless, a year and five months after this dream, at a point when he was deeply emotionally and sexually involved with this young woman and involved in making plans to begin to share an apartment with her, he reported the realization that the abuse had probably actually occurred and that the murdered person in the dream was probably himself. He reported that even as he realized this was true he felt *"my mind wanting to say to me that I am making this up, that I'm crazy, that it never happened."*

At this point he was beside himself with pain at the realization and could not stop sobbing.

Following this he was able to describe how angry he was at his mother for not having protected him. She had worked days and had left him at home alone with his alcoholic father. (When she was home she was often unavailable as well, spending what seemed to him an eternity in the bathroom. She suffered with colitis, to such a degree that Carl worried about her and felt that he had to take care of her rather than the other way around.)

There were associations to his terror of his father's rages. He also reported memories of being taken to bars by his father and left to sit alone as his father drank himself into oblivion.

As we pursued this material he came to the realization that, whereas in the past he thought his homosexual fantasies were basically about depersonalizing others to make them less threatening, he *now* felt that the essential impulse actually had to do with the desire to murder someone, that he really wanted to murder his sexual partners after humiliating them and forcing sex on them. He now understood that this was the basis for his terror that he might lose control of himself if he really let himself feel his feelings or desires or even talk about them in treatment.

With much emotion he also related that the one time in his life he expressed his anger to his father, which was when Carl himself was in college, his father died two weeks later. This convinced him that his anger was lethal, especially since he believed he did want to kill his father.

There were fleeting and disturbing thoughts that maybe he had actually killed someone and had repressed it, even as he insisted he was sure he had not.

Then he reported a sense that his father had threatened to murder him if he were to have told anyone about the abuse, even as he continued to question whether any of this had happened. He expressed feelings of terror even now about telling me, and fear I would not believe him, as he believed his mother would not have believed him had he told her then.

Later he reported a realization of the degree to which his own fantasied scenarios and the scenarios with his sexual partners actually replicated his own experiences with his father, with himself in the role of either abuser or victim, and a sense that his father had pulled his (Carl's) hair, which he linked to his own hair fetish.

During this period, over three years into the work, as he and his girlfriend were on the verge of beginning to live together, Carl reported the following dream: *"A nuclear bomb was supposed to go off imminently, at 1:30 p. m. I was in a state of terrified anticipation. Then 1:30 passed and I realized that if it had not gone off it would not go off. I was relieved and ecstatic to realize the danger was over."*

In a session after this one, Carl retrieved a memory of a recurring nightmare he used to have as a child:

"I was out in my back yard . . . this must have been when I was five or six . . . something was coming towards me and I could never quite see what it was. In my head it was a monster. I became paralyzed and couldn't move. I started screaming for my mother.

She said she was busy and would be there in a minute. I kept screaming and she didn't come. The thing came up and touched me. Then I became 'outside' myself and saw the results. I had been turned into letters of the alphabet on the floor that were sizzling and burning. . . . And I was watching."

Associations at this point included the recognition of a fear that I might not be there for him as his mother had not been then, as he thus began to explore aspects of his experience previously too terrifying to acknowledge, even to himself.

Following this Carl asked if he could increase his sessions from once to twice a week. Sometime later he asked to use the couch.

After living together for about two years (now in the sixth year of our work), Carl and his girlfriend got married. At this time he reported that sex with his wife was more intense than anything he had ever experienced with a man and that it often brought him to tears.

He noted that sometimes he was *"afraid to have sex with my wife because of all the feelings. . . . I am afraid I will flip into a homosexual fantasy, or if I let myself be present and feel the feelings I feel a lot of grief, a lot of pain, it's too intense."*

In this context he reported the following dream:

"I was walking around with this man with whom I knew I had a sexual relationship and he had control over me. Part of me was afraid of him and wanted to get away and another part was very attracted to him and didn't want to get away. Then the dream shifted and he wasn't there anymore, and I was basically raping a man. I had him down on the stomach, was grabbing him by the hair and talking roughly to him. And I had something in my hand like a short pipe that I was forcing up his anus and basically raping him with. I had no feelings for this man, no empathy, no feeling for what I was doing."

And another dream, also disturbing:

"I was on top of this cliff. I don't know what was going on and why I was doing it. There was a man and a woman. I grabbed the man and threw him off to kill him. After I did that and I knew he was dead I did the same thing with the woman, only she fell into water and was still alive. So I went down and held her head under water. She was struggling until I drowned her. I walked away and

didn't feel any remorse. I knew I had to do it. I didn't know why. The only thing I felt was fear I would get caught. Then this flood started to happen and I was very relieved because I knew the bodies would be washed away and my chance of being caught was much less. Then I went into a machine like a relaxation machine or sauna. Then someone came and said my time was up. I came out and saw all these people and didn't want to be recognized. I snuck out hoping not to be noticed."

His associations were:

"The man who was controlling me I thought was my father. I escaped him but I didn't escape him because at least in my mind I am doing what he did. I think part of avoiding sex with my wife during the holiday was because you weren't around. All this stuff was happening in my dreams and I didn't want to open more up when I didn't have you around to talk about it with. I feel any sexual contact opens it up because my defenses aren't working. I feel so unsafe and so scared being that intimate, and being that vulnerable and that close. . . . I think there is a lot of grief coming to the surface."

In a session shortly after Carl reported how eager he had been to come to his session and how *"On the way here I had a fantasy you had been killed and wouldn't be here."* He began to cry, as he continued, *"I got really upset wondering who am I going to talk to about this. All these thoughts went through my head really fast. Then I thought, 'this is crazy thinking.'"*

Ironically (or perhaps he was tuning into something), I became quite ill and was out of work for about six weeks following this. The timing could not have been worse.

When I returned, as I tried to explore his reaction to my illness and absence he insisted that, though he had been very concerned about me, he had been able to cope with it. The situation was further compounded by the fact that summer vacation was approaching, which meant yet another interruption, this time of four weeks.

During this period he and his wife began to make plans to move to another city, something they had both hoped to do for a long time.

We discussed this, how it related to my illness and absence, to fact of the coming summer vacation, to his experience of having to confront my vulnerability. He said he could see that this might be related in some way to his decision to leave New York but he remained firm about following through on his plan, which was to move in about six months.

As much as I tried to address his feelings, he seemed to think it was now my issue and not his. He worried I would try to hold him back. He wanted my understanding and approval. He had decided he was working toward terminating. I felt interrupting our work at this time would be premature. We seemed to be in a stalemate.

Several months after summer vacation, despite my continued efforts, I felt we still had not been able to deal adequately with the issue of my illness and its impact. The fact that I became ill immediately following his fantasy that I had died seemed particularly problematic, given his concern that his father had died the one time he had expressed his anger towards him.

In this context I began to wonder whether it might be useful to review with him some of the dreams he had reported just prior to my illness. I explored this idea with him and asked what his thoughts were, saying I myself was not sure whether this would be a good idea or not. He said he was nervous about it, but nevertheless he wanted to review the dreams. He said also that he wanted to wait until the next session to prepare himself. I felt we should discuss it further and in the following session we did. Though I had anticipated that this would be something we might discuss over some period of time, he seemed very taken with the prospect and wanted to proceed immediately. At this point it seemed important to respect his wish and I shared my notes with him.

As it turned out he had not remembered these dreams at all. The first was the dream in which he was under another man's control and afraid and attracted at the same time. Then he was raping the man with the pipe, with no feeling. The second was the dream in which he killed the man and the woman and felt no remorse. He reported that once he read these dreams they came back immediately. In fact, they stirred much emotion, and he noted they were *"powerfully disturbing."*

A few sessions later he reported a dream:

"I was in a house with my family. We just had some kind of family celebration which we were enjoying. Then it got late and everybody decided they were going to bed. My brothers went upstairs. I was just about to get ready to go up to go to bed. I saw my mother standing in the next room. She was wearing a bathrobe with nothing under it and the bathrobe was wide open. My eyes went right to her vagina. We both looked at each other with shock. Then she kept going. I went upstairs to go to sleep and my brothers were getting high on drugs and playing loud music. I was angry. I felt like a jerk not being able to stand up for my own needs. I felt angry and annoyed for not saying anything. It crossed my mind to go tell my mother what they were doing but I decided not to. At the end of the dream they were talking about going to Europe. At that point I got a little excited about the idea and felt glad for them."

He added, *"The image of seeing my mother naked and looking at her vagina was pretty weird."*

He continued, saying that for the past two mornings he had woken up with a powerful urge to masturbate and that he had been feeling angry the past couple of days. He had had a flash of feeling that he was really angry at me, which surprised him.

"I can't even remember exactly what I was thinking. I guess I am still feeling kind of angry at you. . . . I have been thinking about the dream from your notes about killing a man and a woman and not feeling any remorse. I remember a session a long time ago when I came in and instead of lying down on the couch as usual I violently picked up the chair and moved it two feet closer to you and said that I had to sit close and see you from close, and I just ranted and raved at you the whole session and you said nothing.

"The next session I walked in and I paused between the chair and the couch and as I hesitated you said, 'Chair? Couch? Or lap?' Then I laughed and I got on the couch. It hit home immediately because what's under all my anger is my neediness. The anger is about not being taken care of.

"Now I am confused. I used to be clear that I need to vent the anger to let go of it, but now I think if what it's about is feeling needy and vulnerable and letting myself be comforted then venting my anger won't solve it. I have an image now of a guy I know who

*was in treatment and ranted and raved for months and never got
better. He wouldn't let anybody in. He wouldn't be vulnerable.
When I said 'vulnerable' the image of my mother came back. I can't
imagine anything more vulnerable for her. To be physically exposed
like that would be the most horrifying thing for her ever. So I was
making her vulnerable in my dream."*

My intervention of presenting him with the dreams he had reported just prior to my illness, and which he had since forgotten,
clearly had had powerful impact. It may well be that the sheer
power was the most critical factor, at a time when he was struggling
with fears about my weakness and vulnerability. What comes to
mind here is the comment of another male patient who was a victim
of sexual abuse, who ultimately began to believe that a kind of
paralysis he experienced in his sessions reflected a state of "self-
castration," which was meant to protect me from the danger of his
acting out sadistically with me. With such patients, establishing
that one is able to take care of oneself can be crucial. In some instances it can be more significant than the actual content of whatever is discussed, even if it is not apparent to analyst or patient at
the time.

Another consideration in the interaction with Carl was the fact I
had been willing to take a risk and how this affected him.

In contrast to the sense of stalemate that had prevailed for so
long, in the months following much new and affectively charged
material emerged. He reported that he had not only been abused by
his father, but also by his siblings. His father had been drunk much
of the time, and mother had been away at work or had been ill, and
so the children were often left at the mercy of each other. There was
a specific memory of an incident in which his brother had threatened to kill him and how terrified he had been.

In this context, as the issue of neglect became focused, I began to
wonder whether he had felt neglected by me, not just during my
absence but also *after* my return to work. Perhaps I had not been
persistent enough in exploring his reactions, even though I thought
I had been. When this finally crystallized in my mind I told him my
thoughts. He was open about the fact that he had not wanted to be
a burden to me when I was sick. I noted that I had certainly been
appreciative then, as well as now, of his concern and caring, but

that if I had not been effective in helping him with his issues then I owed him an apology. I wondered out loud whether he was so used to neglect that it may not even have registered for him, and whether, because I was so vulnerable myself at the time when I was still recuperating, it might have suited my needs not to appreciate his dilemma. He was extremely moved and surprised by my willingness to assume responsibility for possibly failing him and by my caring enough to apologize. He said that no one in his family ever would have responded in that way.

At this point we both recognized the extent to which he leads others to believe he is fine when he is not, and how this serves to perpetuate his sense of feeling neglected. This operates with his wife as well as with me, but *had also been true when he was a child.* His wish was to have the other person know that something was wrong, and to have her respond to his needs, without his having to tell or to ask. Others' failure to demonstrate that they cared enough to figure this out became confirmation of his expectation of disappointment. On this basis he could remain in a constant state of anger, in which he felt himself to be the misunderstood victim.

In this context he reported realizing:

"Maybe I am holding onto the anger as protective. I have been angry at my wife a lot lately, particularly since we had this talk about being more present and talking to each other about what's going on during sex. We haven't had sex since then and I have been angry at her. It's like the pain. When I first started seeing you I had no idea how to express my anger. Now I am pretty good at telling someone when I am angry and if something annoys me, but I haven't gotten real good at being vulnerable and letting people comfort me. Anger protects me. As long as I am angry they can't get through that to get to me. . . . I have this anger barrier. And fantasizing about the men around me is also a barrier to keep from feeling connected with people."

Following this he stated with some excitement that he felt he had another important insight: *"I keep thinking I have to express all this rage and I have to get into it, but **maybe it's the opposite.** I don't want to feel close or vulnerable. I feel numbed out when I am angry and numbed out when I am fantasizing."*

In the following session he reported some dreams he had had the night before:

"A man was dead. But he was standing or sitting. And his body was petrified or putrefied. He was frozen, and he was holding a baby. And the baby was fine. I came and I took the baby from him. The next thing I knew I was by a beach on this huge outside deck. Suddenly I was sick. I remember a week ago I told you a dream in which I was vomiting. I had all this stuff down my throat. Well I started vomiting in this dream too. When I finished vomiting there was this boy climbing the stairs to the deck. He looked like he had some awful disease. I wouldn't let him come up. I didn't want him near me because I didn't want to get it. He was circling the deck and he was vomiting. Then he started chasing me and I ran down to the beach trying to get away from him. It became the beach I went to as a child. I knew I wasn't that far from my grandparents' house. I knew if I could get to their house I would be safe."

He reported that in the dream some adolescent boys then sabotaged his efforts and he woke up at that point feeling physically horrible.

"Then I had another dream with an infant. I remember there was something wrong with the infant. It was like the infant was choking on something. And I had this long thing I was sticking down its throat so I could save it. So it could breathe. Sort of like CPR. I was holding the infant upside down, but I was also putting this thing down its throat."

There were associations to the fact that he has this "gag reflex" and always has to carry sucking candies in case it should start to happen. (He had never mentioned this before.)

He then continued: *"I don't like the insight I had last session about holding onto the anger to avoid closeness. Since then it's very hard to be angry, and I have been aware of a lot of pain that is just there all the time."*

He spoke about wanting to have sex with his wife, but wanting her to be the one to initiate it without him having to ask, and also reported his discovery that *"when I am not into my anger and I am in touch with the grief the masturbating to the homosexual fantasies doesn't work."*

There were further associations to how painful it felt to feel close and intimate and vulnerable. He continued, *"I feel my dreams are getting close to telling me what happened, and I am aware that there is a part of me that still doesn't want to remember."*

There were further associations to the dreams the night before and to prior dreams of vomiting and choking.

"I am horrified by even guessing what all this stuff with the throat might mean. I don't want to think about it, I don't want to guess, I don't want to have any images about it because it is just too awful. . . . I am even resisting it in ways like not being too intimate with my wife because with the anger barrier down the way it is now I know I will be feeling old feelings the minute I get close to her and have sex with her. Right now I would rather avoid sex than feel this stuff."

In the weeks following Carl reported with surprise that he was now finding that the old sadomasochistic homosexual fantasies no longer worked for him, and not simply when he was in touch with his grief, as he had noted earlier. He also reported a heterosexual dream, the first he was aware of ever having in life, and an increasing ability to stand up to people at work, including his boss. In this context he stated that, whereas before he had seen himself as hopelessly defined by his fantasies, he now felt a sense of himself as more complex than he had imagined and a new sense of hope and possibility.

Sometime later, Carl reported the following dream:

*"I am with a group of people standing around a bed with a baby in it. One of the men had a needle and thick leather cord and he was sewing the infant's toes together. It was like we were all in a trance watching this happen. The infant was also in a trance and seemed to feel no pain. Then we all snapped out of it at the same time. And the infant started howling and screaming and we were all horrified. We knew the infant was possessed by the devil. Someone leaned over and tried to undo the sewing but it was so painful to the child that he stopped. Then we all started screaming in unison "Satan be gone!" trying to exorcise the devil. The dream shifted and the child was a toddler, a boy. Somebody had stood him up in front of a toilet. Then he started vomiting, defecating, urinating, all at the same time. Feces were falling on the floor. **All of a sudden his penis***

started to grow. It was erect. It grew to two feet long. That really freaked me out. That is where the dream ended."

He noted that the dream had been so awful and he had not been able to get back to sleep. He stated:

"I feel like the symbol of the penis growing is pretty obvious. It represents sexuality that is being stimulated and my adult self being horrified and out of control. The penis just didn't get erect – it took over. It got humongous. I don't understand about seeing the child as possessed unless I have always seen the child in me as bad. It makes me do bad things. It makes me masturbate to crazy fantasies. It's like I am possessed by it."

Almost echoing June's words, Carl then speculated that *"for someone who was as neglected as I had been as an infant, even sexual abuse might have been welcome and comforting as a relief from being totally isolated."*

This seemed to be a turning point, as Carl finally began to deal with the experience of abuse, with how overwhelming it had been, and with how out of control he felt of both external and internal reality and of his own bodily reactions.

He elaborated that apart from all the tangled feelings about being vulnerable now, it was extremely difficult and painful to really open himself to me, or to his wife, or to anyone, even to people he trusted, because he was also profoundly ashamed of being so messed up. It was easier to say, *"Go away. I don't need you."*

In the sessions following he reported becoming aware of intense feelings of shame about the fact that he had come from parents who were so "messed up" themselves, along with a sense of betraying his parents in trying to differentiate himself from them, even within the privacy of his own mind. In a subsequent session, Carl described realizing for the first time how upset he becomes, and how furious, when his wife works on weekends (like mother).

"That is when I masturbate to fantasies. It's scary to realize I need someone. I can't tolerate feelings of longing, need, or loneliness. I smoke and drink and masturbate to fantasies to get away from those feelings and I get compulsive about all of them so that I shouldn't have to feel the longing. When I do open myself to my wife and feel dependent I feel this wall go up, saying, 'What are you doing, don't be crazy, don't be vulnerable.' It scares me how impor-

tant she is. I don't think I allow myself to feel how important you
[the analyst] are . . . but I realize that I may be denying. It's too
scary to feel dependent on you."

He continued: *"The issue is not just my father, but also my*
mother. I realize it's not just abuse, it's also neglect, and both have
impact. It's not just what was done but also what wasn't done."

He spoke about his fears that his needs won't be met and how he
pushes away so as not to be hurt again. That he could acknowledge
and talk about such feelings in this way seemed a momentous
achievement.

As with Carl, in the treatment of other male victims of homosexual child abuse I have found that, as the identification with the
aggressor became clarified, it began to unravel. These patients, who
before had seemed so formidable, now reported feelings of terror,
vulnerability, and humiliation.

Some other patients, who engaged in voyeuristic and exhibi-
tionistic patterns of behavior, such as peeping into people's homes
or masturbating in bookstores and other public places, reported in
the course of treatment that these behaviors no longer provided the
same "kick." The same applied to fantasies of molesting children or
of engaging in violence even to the point of murder. The main
point, as one of them put it, was that whereas before he had more
or less resigned himself to the fact that he was "ruined" and had
reconciled himself to the belief that he could never have a normal
life, now he understood that he had "choices" as to who he wanted
to be and to become, and that he was not doomed to become an
abuser himself.

In Carl's treatment, as with these other patients, I believe several
factors were crucial. These include the fact that I was emotionally
present and very sensitive to his concerns about me and to his fears
of being overwhelmed by his own experience. I did not intrude by
interpreting or even by asking many questions, but rather allowed
him to reveal only what he wanted as he wanted and to arrive at
insights in his own way and in his own time. These conditions
created the context of safety that he needed before he could dare to
retrieve his memories and arrive at the insights he did. I have found
this to be common with patients who have been sexually abused,
who tend to be sensitive to any form of intrusion, co-option, viola-

tion, or seduction, however subtle, not only by the analyst but also by their own experience and feelings. In this regard I think my deliberately not interpreting the dreams was especially important, allowing him to begin to work things out through the dreams before he was ready to engage them consciously.

My view is that Carl was able to begin dealing with the kind of potentially disorganizing emotions and memories that the defensive identification with the aggressor had apparently helped him to avoid when he was able to trust that I would keep things from getting beyond the point of manageability.

Opening himself to the affects and memories of which he had been so terrified and discovering that he could experience, contain, and talk about such emotions without being overwhelmed and decompensating was healing, integrative, and reassuring in itself. As Carl was increasingly able to contain these formerly dissociated aspects of his experience, he was finally able to grieve the pain of his childhood.

I distinguish this kind of process, which was strengthening in that it enabled Carl to discover that he no longer had to be plagued by the terror of being overwhelmed by his own experience, from an experience of decompensation in the present, which can be traumatic and debilitating. Enabling a patient to discover that he or she can deal with these aspects of experience on his or her own strength and by his or her own choice, at whatever pace he or she desires, rather than depending on the analyst's strength and timing to ultimately carry the work, is ultimately the most reassuring and healing experience of all. This is particularly crucial for sexually abused patients, who so often have been robbed of precisely this kind of experience of sovereignty.

Many questions remain unanswered, and many can be raised. These include how to understand Carl's dramatic and relatively sudden shift in sexual preference. Though I think the working through of his anger towards his mother was crucial here, it may well be that more complete answers will emerge only later.

It may be no surprise that both Carl and June had very intense emotional reactions to reading this chapter. Discussing these reactions became a very productive experience in itself, leading to new insights and to recovery of yet more memories, and also to sharing of some information that they had not been comfortable revealing or acknowledging, to me or themselves, earlier.

For example, June reported for the first time during this process that her masturbation fantasies had often begun with the image of her father and the memory of the pleasure of his touch. Carl reported that my actual absence when I was sick was less traumatic to him than how I looked when I returned. He felt that while I was out it was easy for him to deny that I might have been seriously ill. He noted that when I returned, however, and he was confronted with the fact that I had lost weight and looked weak, he no longer could maintain his denial. At that point he was so alarmed that he felt it was important not to worry me with his concerns, despite my efforts to elicit just this kind of material. (The irony here is that at the time I viewed the weight loss as the only positive thing that had occurred and did not appreciate that it specifically could have been so upsetting to him.)

Even more significantly, however, for patients who often wondered whether their experiences had really happened or had been imagined, the experience of seeing the material in writing seemed to make it tangible in a way that was almost shocking. This allowed for yet new kinds of working through, which I will only touch on briefly here.

June, for example, felt confronted with the degree to which she was still capable of relegating her experience to a kind of unreality, which then rendered her helpless to deal with it. She thus recognized that, even though she had made much progress and could stand up for herself in the present in ways she never would have been able to in the past, if she met with strong resistance she would still become "confused" and wonder whether it was her problem, or decide it was hopeless to fight any further. In effect she began to see how *she let herself* be negated and ignored and ended up questioning herself, or even went "dead" internally, much as she had in relation to her father. There were associations now to her sense of utter dependence, financial as well as emotional, on her father then, to fears she had had then that she would not have been able to survive on her own, as she became aware of the degree to which some of those fears still prevailed in the present. There was also a realization that the denial of her needs and feelings, as well as her real capabilities, extended way beyond the sexual arena in her family. She expressed her current view that, no matter what her parents' problems might have been, these were no excuse for what was done to her and for the fact that they did not "control" themselves and protect her from their pathology. She added that the argument her husband had used in a recent interaction that "this is who I am" was simply no excuse for his behavior now, just as it was no excuse for her parents' actions then.

The process thus launched as we reviewed together the material I had written was intense and extremely productive, as was true for all the patients discussed in this book. I will, however, leave further discussion of the complex impact of the analyst's writing on the patient, on the analyst, and on the process for a future time.

I have tried to demonstrate how a particular way of working that is based on sensitivity to the interactive nature of the analytic field, to the potential for inadvertent enactment, to the importance of what goes on affectively between patient and analyst, and to the need for the analyst to structure a context of adequate safety, can enable patients who have been sexually abused to get to very threatening material and deal with it in ways that would not necessarily be possible in other kinds of contexts. At the same time I have tried to share some of what these patients and I both learned about the impact of sexual abuse, about the complex relation between abuse and desire, and about what can be achieved if one works in this way in such contexts.

Epilogue

MY EFFORT IN THIS BOOK HAS been to try to take the reader into the intimacy of the consulting room to illustrate some ways in which recognition of the interactive nature of the analytic field has profound and radical implications for our thinking about analytic technique, no matter what our theoretical orientation.

In this regard I have focused on how distinguishing between theory of technique, which relates to what we do with awareness and intention, and theory of therapeutic action, which has to do with what is healing in the psychoanalytic interaction whether or not it evolves from our "technique," can enable us to refine psychoanalytic theory, and ourselves as its instrument, so as to expand the limits of what can be achieved with all patients through analytic work.

Stressing the importance of the affective relationship and of unconscious forms of communication and enactment, I have tried to illustrate how the analytic expanse is enlarged, and a unique kind of intimate and moving process is generated, as these dimensions of the interaction, often accessible only through the countertransference, begin to be explicitly acknowledged and addressed. My experience has been that working in this way, at what then becomes the "intimate edge" of the relationship, establishes the conditions that can enable the patient to reach insights on his or her own, and to develop and discover resources and capabilities of which he or she may have been unaware.

Data from the treatment of victims of sexual abuse, anorexic patients, children of alcoholics, as well as many others who might have been considered unanalyzable, was used to demonstrate that, even with patients who have been violated and abused, and for whom cynicism, terror and despair may have long prevailed, working this way can facilitate psychoanalytic engagement and enable patients to feel sufficient hope to reinvest in life and to risk experiencing the profound vulnerability that goes with the awakening of desire.

Focusing on the importance of using countertransference constructively, the value of playfulness, and the role of encounter in the process of working through, I have also tried to illustrate particular ways of using oneself that can be uniquely facilitating. The emphasis is on how to turn potential impasse into analytic opportunity by realizing the unique possibilities of the analytic moment.

Finally, I have tried to convey that being able to facilitate this kind of process is both a privilege and a challenge, that it reflects a very personal and unique process and relationship between each patient and each analyst, and that the kind of reciprocity that is inherent in working this way results in an engagement that inevitably becomes a medium for growth for the analyst as well as the patient.

Notes

[1] Because each of the existing schools of psychoanalytic thought comprises a range of perspectives, affinities often exist across orientations that may not exist within them with regard to conceptions of what the specific implications for technique of these interactive considerations might be.

[2] This may be the basis for the common observation that there is often a discrepancy between how analysts work and how they think they work.

[3] One patient reported dreams in which she was terrorized by the realization that she had to choose between saving the life of a loved one by donating her own vital organs, which meant sacrificing her own life, or letting the loved one die so that she might live.

[4] Freud (1900) writes of the desire for an unsatisfied desire. (See also Lacan, 1958.)

[5] I think this may help us understand why pathology may not be revealed with one analyst, only to emerge in a later treatment.

[6] Since that time (around 1972) I have come to realize that one can go even further with this kind of exploration. For example, one could wonder, Was I reacting to something myself when I looked at the clock? In recent years I have found expanding the exploration in this way to be useful.

[7] My experience is that certain deviations from a rigid frame can be tolerated and absorbed if the internal soundness of the work is maintained. This was particularly evident to me during the course of two pregnancies, when I found it necessary to establish a more flexible schedule with patients. This proved not to interfere with the work but actually stimulated important associations and reactions which might not have occurred or been articulated otherwise. Since then I have also found that with more disturbed patients adding sessions at critical moments or being open to tailoring the structure to the patient's needs, such as having double sessions at stressful times, has been not only helpful but essential in making it possible to sustain an analytic process in the face of high levels of anxiety.

[8] In an earlier publication (Ehrenberg, 1984a) I emphasized that data from a growing literature from all psychoanalytic schools of thought suggest that at times the analyst's own active affective engagement can be crucial, and that this can be constructive in advancing the analytic effort without compromising its integrity At times it may be essential (Winnicott, 1949). I noted there that this body of work makes clear that direct participation by the analyst need not involve the "lending of egos," acting out, manipulation, seduction, mystification, coercion, or any other nonanalytic gesture.
    This literature includes the papers of Rioch (1943); Winnicott (1949, 1969); Fromm-Reichmann (1950, 1952); Gitelson (1950, 1962); Little (1951, 1957); Tauber (1954, 1979); Stone (1954, 1961); Tower (1956); Nacht (1957, 1962); Fairbairn (1958); Wolstein

(1959); Searles (1965, 1979); Guntrip (1969); Singer (1971, 1977); Levenson (1972, 1983); Bird (1972); Ehrenberg (1974, 1975, 1976, 1982a, 1982b, 1984a, 1985a); Sandler (1976); McDougall (1979); Klauber (1981); Feiner (1979, 1982, 1983); Bollas (1983); Hoffman (1983); Symington (1983); and Tustin (1988), among many others.

⁹ Tustin's (1988) comment about the necessity for a "therapist who is a lively active presence who will not be canceled out" comes to mind. (The interaction described above took place around 1970.)

¹⁰ This brings to mind a moment when another patient reported a terrifying image of being under a tombstone and unable to lift it. My comment, *"Why try to lift it, why not just slide out from under?"* seemed to be similarly liberating.

¹¹ Tower (1956) makes a similar point. Describing an incident when finally reacting to the patient's "abusive resistance" seemed to turn the work around, she comments as follows:

> One could say I was irritated with the patient and missed her hour because of aggression which was of course true. But the real countertransference problem was not that. Actually, my acting out behavior was reality-based and brought a resolution to the countertransference problem which was that I had been patient with her too long. . . . This prolonged abusive resistance need not have lasted so long had I been freer to be more aggressive in the face of it. (p. 238)

Similarly, Bollas (1983), describing what happened when he finally "stood up" to a particular patient, writes:

> My previous analysis of [the patient's] anxiety and his defenses against anxiety, although correct, had never reached the core of the issue, and later he told me that he rather despaired that I would ever speak up for myself. When I

did, instead of burdening him with a sense of guilt, quite
the opposite happened, as the fact that up until then I had
not personally resisted his created environment had left him
feeling doomed and monstrous. (p. 25)

[12] I will not attempt to review the growing literature on sequelae
of abuse, because my focus here is on the treatment process itself
and what specifically emerged in the course of my work with these
patients. However, the findings reported here are consistent with
those in this literature and, I believe, expand upon them, as will
become evident as the details of these treatments unfold.

[13] This is a correction of the ages noted in an earlier publication
(Ehrenberg, 1987).

[14] On reading this June noted that when father came into her
room, *"I took advantage of it. The arousal was exciting and plea-
surable."*

References

Abelin, E. L. (1971). The role of the father in the separation-individuation Process. In J. B. McDevitt & C. F. Settlage (Eds.), *Separation-individuation: Essays in honor of Margaret S. Mahler* (pp. 229–253). New York: International Universities Press.

Abelin, E. L. (1975). Some further observations and comments on the earliest role of the father. *International Journal of Psycho-Analysis, 56:* 293–302.

Alexander, F. (1956). *Psychoanalysis and psychotherapy.* New York: Norton.

Bateson, G. (1972). A theory of play and fantasy. In G. Bateson, *Steps to an ecology of mind* (pp. 177–193). New York: Ballantine.

Becker, E. (1973). *The denial of death.* New York: Free Press.

Beres, D., & Arlow, J. A. (1974). Fantasy and identification in empathy. *Psychoanalytic Quarterly, 43:* 26–50.

Bion, W. R. (1967). *Second thoughts.* New York: Aronson.

Bion, W. R. (1983). *Attention and interpretation.* New York: Aronson.

Bird, B. (1972). Notes on transference: Universal phenomenon and hardest part of analysis. *Journal of the American Psychoanalytic Association, 20:* 267–301.

Bollas, C. (1983). Expressive uses of the countertransference: Notes to the patient from oneself. *Contemporary Psychoanalysis, 19:* 1–34.

Bollas, C. (1987). *The shadow of the object.* New York: Columbia University Press.

Breuer, J. (1895). Case I: Miss Anna O. In J. Strachey (Ed. & Trans.), *The standard edition of the complete psychological works of Sigmund Freud* (vol. 2, pp. 21–47). New York: Norton.

Buber, M. (1957a). Distance and relation. *Psychiatry, 20:* 2.

Buber, M. (1957b). Elements of the interhuman. *Psychiatry, 20:* 2.

Buber, M. (1958). *I and thou.* New York: Scribner's.

Ehrenberg, B. (1980). The repair of the unconscious. *Contemporary Psychoanalysis 16:* 249–257.

Ehrenberg, D. B. (1974). The "intimate edge" in therapeutic relatedness. *Contemporary Psychoanalysis, 10:* 423–437.

Ehrenberg, D. B. (1975). The quest for intimate relatedness. *Contemporary Psychoanalysis, 11:* 320–331.

Ehrenberg, D. B. (1976). The "intimate edge" and the "third area." *Contemporary Psychoanalysis, 12:* 489–496.

Ehrenberg, D. B. (1982a). Psychoanalytic engagement: The transaction as primary data. *Contemporary Psychoanalysis, 18:* 535–555.

Ehrenberg, D. B. (1982b). Discussion of Conference on Approaches in Psychotherapy. *Contemporary Psychoanalysis, 18:* 522–534.

Ehrenberg, D. B. (1984a). Psychoanalytic engagement II: Affective considerations. *Contemporary Psychoanalysis, 20:* 560–583.

Ehrenberg, D. B. (1984b). Reply to discussions of "Psychoanalytic engagement II." *Contemporary Psychoanalysis, 20:* 595–599.

Ehrenberg, D. B. (1985a). Countertransference resistance. *Contemporary Psychoanalysis, 21:* 563–576.

Ehrenberg, D. B. (1985b, August 24). The dialectics of desire. In *Illusion and desire: Lacan and the ethics of psychoanalysis.* Panel discussion presented at the annual convention of the American Psychological Association, Div. 39, Los Angeles, CA.

Ehrenberg, D. B. (1987). Abuse and desire: A case of father-daughter incest. *Contemporary Psychoanalysis, 23:* 593–604.

Ehrenberg, D. B. (1990). Playfulness in the psychoanalytic relationship. *Contemporary Psychoanalysis 26:* 74–95.

Fairbairn, W. R. D. (1958). On the nature and aims of psycho-analytical treatment. *International Journal of Psycho-Analysis, 39:* 374–385.

Farber, L. (1966). *The ways of the will.* New York: Basic Books.

Feiner, A. H. (1970). Toward an understanding of the experience of inauthenticity. *Contemporary Psychoanalysis, 7:* 64–83.

Feiner, A. H. (1979). Countertransference and the anxiety of influence. In L. Epstein & A. H. Feiner (Eds.), *Countertransference.* New York: Aronson.

Feiner, A. H. (1983). On the facilitation of the therapeutic symbiosis. *Contemporary Psychoanalysis, 19:* 673–689.

Ferenczi, S. (1933). Confusion of tongues between adults and the child. In S. Ferenczi (1955), *Final contributions to the problems and methods of psycho-analysis* (pp. 87–101). London: Hogarth.

Freud, S. (1900). Interpretation of dreams. In J. Strachey (Ed. & Trans.), *The standard edition of the complete psychological works of Sigmund Freud* (vols. 4 & 5). New York: Norton.

Freud, S. (1915a [1914]). Observations on transference-love: Further recommendations on the technique of psychoanalysis. In J. Strachey (Ed. & Trans.), *The standard edition of the complete psychological works of Sigmund Freud* (vol. 12, pp. 159–71). New York: Norton.

Freud, S. (1915b). The unconscious. In J. Strachey (Ed. & Trans.), *The standard edition of the complete psychological works of Sigmund Freud* (vol. 14, pp. 159–215). New York: Norton.

Fromm, E. (1941). *Escape from freedom.* New York: Holt, Rinehart & Winston.

Fromm-Reichmann, F. (1939). Transference problems in schizophrenics. *Psychoanalytic Quarterly, 8:* 412–26.

Fromm-Reichmann, F. (1950). *Principles of intensive psychotherapy.* Chicago: University of Chicago Press.

Fromm-Reichmann, F. (1952). Some aspects of psychoanalytic psychotherapy with schizophrenia. In E. B. Brody & C. F. Redlich (Eds.), *Psychotherapy with schizophrenics.* New York: International Universities Press.

Gill, M. (1979). The analysis of the transference. *Journal of the American Psychoanalytic Association, 27:* 267–288 (Supplement).

Gill, M. (1982a). *Analysis of transference* (vol. I). New York: International Universities Press.

Gill, M. (1982b). Merton Gill: An interview. *Psychoanalytic Review, 69:* 167–190.

Gill, M. (1983). The interpersonal paradigm and the degree of the therapist's involvement. *Contemporary Psychoanalysis, 19:* 200–237.

Gill, M. (1984). Psychoanalysis and psychotherapy: A revision. *International Review of Psycho-Analysis, 2:* 161–180.

Gill, M. (1985). The interactional aspect of transference: Range of application. In E. A. Schwaber (Ed.), *The transference in psychotherapy: Clinical management.* New York: International Universities Press.

Gill, M. (1991). Indirect suggestion: A response to Oremland's *Interpretation and interaction.* In J. D. Oremland (Ed.), *Interpretation and interaction: Psychoanalysis or psychotherapy.* Hillsdale, NJ: Analytic Press.

Gitelson, M. (1952). The emotional position of the analyst in the psychoanalytic situation. *International Journal of Psycho-Analysis, 33:* 1–10.

Gitelson, M. (1962). The curative factors in psychoanalysis. *International Journal of Psycho-Analysis, 43:* 194–205.

Grinberg, L. (1962). On a specific aspect of countertransference due to the patient's projective identification. *International Journal of Psycho-Analysis, 43:* 436–440.

Grinberg, L. (1979). Countertransference and projective counteridentification. In L. Epstein & A. Feiner (Eds.), *Countertransference.* New York: Aronson.

Grotstein, J. S. (1981). *Splitting and projective identification.* New York: Aronson.

Guntrip, H. (1969). *Schizoid phenomena, object relations and the self.* New York: International Universities Press.

Heimann, P. (1950). On countertransference. *International Journal of Psycho-Analysis, 31:* 81-84.

Hoffman, I. Z. (1983). The patient as interpreter of the analyst's experience. *Contemporary Psychoanalysis, 19:* 389-422.

Hoffman, I. Z. (1991). Discussion: Towards a social-constructivist view of the psychoanalytic situation. *Dialogues, 1:* 74-105.

Hoffman, I. Z. (1992). Expressive participation and psychoanalytic discipline. *Contemporary Psychoanalysis, 28:* 1-15.

Khan, M. (1969). On symbiotic omnipotence. In M. Khan (1974), *The privacy of the self.* New York: International Universities Press.

Klauber, J. (1981). *Difficulties in the analytic encounter.* New York: Aronson.

Lacan, J. (1953). The function and field of speech and language in psychoanalysis. In J. Lacan (1977), *Ecrits* (pp. 30-113) (A. Sheridan, Trans.). New York: Norton.

Lacan, J. (1958). The direction of the treatment and the principles of its power. In J. Lacan (1977), *Ecrits* (pp. 226-280) (A. Sheridan, Trans.). New York: Norton.

Laing, R. D. (1965). Mystification, confusion and conflict. In I. Boszormenyi-Nagi & J. L. Framo (Eds.), *Intensive family therapy.* New York: Harper & Row.

Langs, R. (1976). *The bipersonal field.* New York: Aronson.

Levenson, E. A. (1972). *The fallacy of understanding.* New York: Basic Books.

Levenson, E. A. (1983). *The ambiguity of change.* New York: Basic Books.

Lipton, S. (1977a). The advantages of Freud's technique as shown in his analysis of the Rat Man. *International Journal of Psycho-Analysis, 58:* 255-274.

Lipton, S. (1977b). Clinical observations on resistance to the transference. *International Journal of Psycho-Analysis 58:* 463-472.

Lipton, S. (1983). A critique of so-called standard psychoanalytic technique. *Contemporary Psychoanalysis, 19:* 35-46.

Little, M. (1951). Countertransference and the patient's response to it. *International Journal of Psycho-Analysis, 32:* 32-40.

Little, M. (1957). "R" – The analyst's total response to his patient's needs. *International Journal of Psycho-Analysis, 38:* 240-254.

Loewald, H. (1960). On the therapeutic action of psychoanalysis. *International Journal of Psycho-Analysis, 41:* 16-33.

Mahler, M. S. (1967). On human symbiosis and the vicissitudes of individuation. *Journal of the American Psychoanalytic Association, 15:* 740–763.

Mahler, M. S., Pine F., & Bergman, A. (1975). *The psychological birth of the human infant.* New York: Basic Books.

Maldonado, J. L. (1987). Narcissism and unconscious communication. *International Journal of Psycho-Analysis, 68:* 379–387.

McDougall, J. (1979). Primitive communication and the use of countertransference. In L. Epstein & A. H. Feiner (Eds.), *Countertransference.* New York: Aronson.

Nacht, S. (1957). Technical remarks on the handling of the transference neurosis. *International Journal of Psycho-Analysis, 38:* 196–203.

Nacht, S. (1962). The curative factors in psychoanalysis. *International Journal of Psycho-Analysis, 43:* 206–211.

Ogden, T. (1979). On projective identification. *International Journal of Psycho-Analysis, 60:* 357–373.

Racker, H. (1957). The meaning and uses of countertransference. *Psychoanalytic Quarterly, 26:* 303–357.

Racker, H. (1968). *Transference and countertransference.* London: Hogarth Press.

Rank, O. (1929). *Will therapy.* New York: Norton, 1978.

Reich, A. (1951). On counter-transference. *International Journal of Psycho-Analysis, 32:* 25–31.

Reich, A. (1960). Further remarks on counter-transference. *International Journal of Psycho-Analysis, 41:* 389–395.

Rioch, J. M. (1943). The transference phenomenon in psychoanalytic therapy. *Psychiatry, 6:* 147–156.

Sandler, J. (1976). Countertransference and role responsiveness. *International Review of Psycho-Analysis 3:* 43–47.

Schachtel, E. G. (1959). *Metamorphosis.* New York: Basic Books.

Searles, H. (1965). *Collected papers on schizophrenia and related subjects.* New York: International Universities Press.

Searles, H. (1975). The patient as therapist to his analyst. In H. Searles (1979), *Countertransference and related subjects. Selected papers.* New York: International Universities Press.

Searles, H. (1979). *Countertransference and related subjects. Selected papers.* New York: International Universities Press.

Searles, H. (1990). Unconscious identification. In L. B. Boyer and P. Giovacchini (Eds.) *Master clinicians: On treating the regressed patient.* Northvale, NJ: Aronson.

Singer, E. (1965). *Key concepts in psychotherapy.* New York: Random House.

Singer, E. (1971). The patient aids the analyst: Some clinical and theoretical observations. In B. Landis & E. Tauber (Eds.), *In the name of life.* New York: Holt, Rinehart & Winston.

Singer, E. (1977). The fiction of analytic anonymity. In K. Frank (Ed.), *The human dimension in psychoanalytic practice* (pp. 181–192). New York: Grune & Stratton.

Stern, Daniel (1983). The early development of schemas of self, other and "self with others." In J. Lichtenberg & S. Kaplan (Eds.), *Reflections on self psychology* (pp. 49–84). Hillsdale, NJ: The Analytic Press.

Stern, Daniel (1985). *The interpersonal world of the infant: A view from psychoanalysis and developmental psychology.* New York: Basic Books.

Stone, L. (1954). The widening scope of indications for psychoanalysis. *Journal of the American Psychoanalytic Association 2:* 567–594.

Stone, L. (1961). *The psychoanalytic situation.* New York: International Universities Press.

Sullivan, H. S. (1953). *The interpersonal theory of psychiatry.* New York: Norton.

Symington, N. (1983). The analyst's act of freedom as agent of therapeutic change. *International Review of Psycho-Analysis, 10:* 283–291.

Tauber, E. S. (1954). Exploring the therapeutic use of countertransference data. *Psychiatry, 17:* 331–336.

Tauber, E. S. (1979). Countertransference re-examined. In L. Epstein & A. H. Feiner (Eds.), *Countertransference.* New York: Aronson.

Tower, L. (1956). Countertransference. *Journal of the American Psychoanalytic Association, 4:* 224–255.

Tustin, F. (1988). Psychotherapy with children who cannot play. *International Review of Psycho-Analysis, 15:* 93–106.

Widlocher, D. (1985). The wish for identification and structural effects in the work of Freud. *The International Journal of Psycho-Analysis, 66:* 31–47.

Winnicott, D. W. (1935). The manic defense. In D. W. Winnicott (1958), *Collected papers: Through paediatrics to psycho-analysis.* London: Tavistock Publications.

Winnicott, D. W. (1949). Hate in the countertransference. In D. W. Winnicott (1958), *Collected papers: Through paediatrics to psycho-analysis.* London: Tavistock Publications.

Winnicott, D. W. (1951). Transitional objects and transitional phenomena. In D. W. Winnicott (1958), *Collected papers: Through paediatrics to psycho-analysis.* London: Tavistock Publications.

Winnicott, D. W. (1956). On transference. *International Journal of Psycho-Analysis, 37:* 386–388.

Winnicott, D. W. (1963a). Dependence in infant-care, in child-care, and in the psycho-analytic setting. In D. W. Winnicott (1965), *The maturational processes and the facilitating environment.* New York: International Universities Press.

Winnicott, D. W. (1963b). The development of the capacity for concern. In D. W. Winnicott (1965), *The maturational processes and the facilitating environment.* New York: International Universities Press.

Winnicott, D. W. (1965). *The maturational processes and the facilitating environment.* New York: International Universities Press.

Winnicott, D. W. (1967). Mirror-role of mother and family in child development. In D. W. Winnicott (1971), *Playing and reality.* New York: Basic Books.

Winnicott, D. W. (1969). The use of an object and relating through identifications. In D. W. Winnicott (1971), *Playing and reality.* New York: Basic Books.

Winnicott, D. W. (1971). *Playing and reality.* New York: Basic Books.

Wolstein, B. (1959). *Countertransference.* New York: Grune & Stratton.

Wolstein, B. (1971). *Human psyche in psychoanalysis.* Springfield, IL: Charles C Thomas.

Index

CASE INDEX

GENERAL INDEX